Daniel E. Petree
10-5-2010

THE MODERN
BABYLON

THE MODERN BABYLON

By Frances Swaggart

Jimmy Swaggart Ministries
P.O. Box 262550
Baton Rouge, Louisiana 70826-2550
www.jsm.org
E-mail: info@jsm.org
(225) 768-8300

ISBN 978-0-9769530-6-7
09-071 • COPYRIGHT © 2006 **World Evangelism Press**®
P.O. Box 262550 • Baton Rouge, Louisiana 70826-2550
All rights reserved. Printed and bound in U.S.A.
No part of this publication may be reproduced in any form or by any means
without the publisher's prior written permission.

TABLE OF CONTENTS

CHAPTER ONE	1
CHAPTER TWO	13
CHAPTER THREE	23
CHAPTER FOUR	35
CHAPTER FIVE	47
CHAPTER SIX	59
CHAPTER SEVEN	71
CHAPTER EIGHT	79
CHAPTER NINE	87
CHAPTER TEN	97
CHAPTER ELEVEN	105
CHAPTER TWELVE	115
CHAPTER THIRTEEN	125
CHAPTER FOURTEEN	133
CHAPTER FIFTEEN	141
CHAPTER SIXTEEN	151
CHAPTER SEVENTEEN	159
CHAPTER EIGHTEEN	167

INTRODUCTION

For many years, the Catholic Church was the only Christian Church until the Protestant Reformation. Even today, when the secular world thinks of Christianity, most automatically associate it with Catholicism. While such is understandable for the world, it should be very alarming to true Christians. Why? — because the Protestant Reformation brought the Church back to the Word of God. Before this, the people were told that they needed priests and popes to interpret the Scriptures, and copies of the Bible were not put in the hands of the common layman. Therefore, those who refused to break away from the Roman Catholic Church at this time refused the Light of God's Word and chose to remain in darkness. Quite prophetically, secular history even called this period of time in which Catholicism ruled, *"The Dark Ages"*. No constructive progress was made because the Light of the Gospel was hidden.

This brings us to the purpose of this book because what we are seeing in the modern Church is a very disturbing trend, a trend which is essentially the reversal of the Reformation! The Church today is rapidly embracing Roman Catholicism's darkness once again! Not only did the Catholic religion withhold the Scriptures for their own purposes, namely the acquisition of wealth and power, but they also majored in pagan religious traditions in order to lure the pagan worshippers into their sheepfold as well. The Roman Catholic Church was, in fact, the first mega-church. Where today's mega-church uses advanced marketing techniques and the latest fads in pop culture to attract the masses, the Roman Catholic Church implemented pagan culture to draw in the unchurched of that day. This way the pagans did not feel threatened and, yet, could also gain something extra — the blessing of the

"Christian" Church.

So, where does Babylon fit in? The Bible speaks of a city called Babylon which exemplified paganism, paganism being any and all forms of rebellion against God and His Way. We actually see the spirit of Babylon in many forms — a great city, an adulterous woman, a mysterious religion, a high tower, etc. But regardless of its image, there always seemed to be something in the hearts of men that desired to see *"Babylon"* succeed, and in his deepest heart, man inevitably manages to find the faith to believe it will. Why? — because man's fatal flaw is faith in himself, and *"Babylon"* is always the collective incarnation of man's creative ideas and endeavors, whether scientific or religious, which reaches for greatness, or even for God. In other words, Babylon is the zenith of men's works, while true Christianity respects nothing but God's Grace! Catholicism, having so efficiently incorporated pagan traditions and works into their Church, is indeed a modern Babylon!

"Babylon" is always associated with *"mystery"* as well, stemming from the entire enigma surrounding man's attempt at greatness. The mystery has always remained because, while time and again man is fooled by his prideful heart, in all reality, he is actually unable to achieve it! As we will bring out, Catholicism clearly shows her true Babylonian spirit in this regard as well, given that she is full of mystery and intrigue. In true Christianity, Truth is readily revealed to all.

"And upon her forehead was a name written, MYSTERY, BABYLON THE GREAT, THE MOTHER OF HARLOTS AND ABOMINATIONS OF THE EARTH" (Rev. 17:5).

CHAPTER ONE

Is the Roman Catholic Church Christian or is it pagan? To answer this question, we can begin by returning to the time period shortly after the flood. It was at this time that men began to migrate from the east. *"And it came to pass that when they journeyed from the east, that they found a plain in the land of Shinar; and they dwelt there"* (Gen. 11:2).

The phrase *"from the east"* can also mean *"in the east,"* the latter probably being the way it should read. It was in this land of Shinar that the city of Babylon was built. It was later called Mesopotamia. *"And Cush begat Nimrod: he began to be a mighty one in the earth. He was a mighty hunter before the Lord: wherefore it is said, even as Nimrod the mighty hunter before the Lord. And the beginning of his kingdom was Babel, and Erech, and Accad, and Calneh, in the land of Shinar"* (Gen. 10:8-10). Nimrod was introduced here, and he engineered the first organized rebellion against God.

While Nimrod may have been a ***"mighty one in the earth,"*** he was not mighty in heaven. The use of the phrase ***"before the Lord,"*** with regard to Nimrod, actually means ***"in opposition to the Lord."*** ***"Before"*** was the translation of a Hebrew word meaning ***"against the Lord."*** Nimrod was the builder of the Tower of Babel, which was the heart of this organized rebellion. The Tower of Babel was dedicated to the false gods of the sun and other heavenly bodies. Nimrod, it is said, even positioned a zodiac at the top of the Tower of Babel to help the Babylonians interpret the divine will of these gods. Not surprisingly, similar architecture and symbolism were later used by others in the Middle East and among the Incas, Mayans, and Aztecs.

JERUSALEM AND BABYLON

Down through the history of the Work of God, wherever God

has a corporate witness on the earth, Satan has a Babylon to mar and corrupt that witness. When God connects his name with a city on earth, **Jerusalem**, then **Babylon** takes the form of a city. When God connects His name with a Church, then Babylon takes the form of a corrupt religious system called, *"the great whore,"* the mother of abominations, etc.

"And there came one of the seven angels which had the seven vials, and talked with me, saying unto me, Come hither; I will shew unto thee the judgment of the great whore that sitteth upon many waters: With whom the kings of the earth have committed fornication, and the inhabitants of the earth have been made drunk with the wine of her fornication. So he carried me away in the Spirit into the wilderness: and I saw a woman sit upon a scarlet coloured beast, full of names of blasphemy, having seven heads and ten horns. And the woman was arrayed in purple and scarlet colour, and decked with gold and precious stones and pearls, having a golden cup in her hand full of abominations and filthiness of her fornication: And upon her forehead was a name written, MYSTERY, BABYLON THE GREAT, THE MOTHER OF HARLOTS AND ABOMINATIONS OF THE EARTH" (Rev. 17:1-5).

Satan's Babylon is always seen as the instrument molded and fashioned by his hand for the purpose of counteracting the Divine operations of God. Whether in the Old Testament account of Israel or in the Church now, Israel and Babylon are seen as opposites. Babylon has always stood for every false religion, every false doctrine, and every false way. This is why it is referred to as *"the great whore — mother of harlots and abominations of the earth."* The cities represent two major themes of the Bible: ***"Jerusalem,"*** where God has chosen to place His name and ***"Babylon,"*** which is the opposite of everything pertaining to the Lord.

NIMROD

Not only was Nimrod against the true God, he was also a priest of devil worship and heathenism of the worst kind, a type of nature and celestial adoration. Being ***"against God"*** and ***"against the***

ways of the Lord," also made him against those who followed the Lord. He ***"hunted"*** them down, possibly even killing those who worshipped Jehovah. Nimrod, the king and founder of Babylon, was the religious leader as well as the political leader of Babylon. He stood as priest-king and from him descended a line of priest-kings — each standing at the head of the occultic Babylonian mystery religion. This line continued down to the days of Belshazzar, of whom we read about in the Bible. The Bible tells us of the feast he had in Babylon when the mysterious handwriting appeared on the wall. This gathering was not a mere social gathering but a religious gathering as well.

The filthy and abominable practices of the occasion were part of the Babylonian ceremonies of the mystery religion, of which Belshazzar was head over at that time. *"They drank wine, and praised the gods of gold, and of silver, of brass, of iron, of wood, and of stone"* (Dan. 5:4). Adding to the blasphemy of the occasion, they drank their wine from the Holy Vessels of the Lord. The mixing of the Holy Vessels used in heathen worship brought God's swift judgment upon Belshazzar. **Babylon was marked for doom.** The ancient city is now in ruins, uninhabited, and desolate. *"Therefore the wild beasts of the desert with the wild beasts of the islands shall dwell there, and the owls shall dwell therein: and it shall be no more inhabited for ever; neither shall it be dwelt in from generation to generation"* (Jer. 50:39). *"Then shalt thou say, O Lord, thou has spoken against this place, to cut it off, that none shall remain in it, neither man nor beast, but that it shall be desolate for ever"* (Jer. 51:62).

SEMIRAMIS, WIFE OF NIMROD

According to tradition, when Nimrod died, his body was cut into pieces and distributed to different areas of the earth. The Babylonian religion, however, did not end at Nimrod's death. Nimrod's wife, Semiramis, who was obviously inspired by Satan, took over the leadership and actually further developed the system. Semiramis declared that Nimrod had now become The Sun God, which made her *"Queen."* Later, Queen Semiramis gave birth to an illegitimate son named *"Tammuz."* She claimed that her flawless son, Tammuz, was Nimrod reborn, that he was supernaturally conceived, and that he was the promised seed, the *"savior."* Tammuz was not the only one to be worshipped. Queen Semiramis was to be worshipped as well, now being the mother of the gods.

This unholy family was used as puppets in Satan's hand to produce a common theme among various false religions. Sadly, these religions often appeared true because the **true Faith of Abraham, Isaac, and Jacob looked for a Promised Seed**. Among other beliefs of the Babylonians, the lie of Nimrod's family filled the world when the Babylonian people were scattered, **so men had been worshipping a divine mother and god-child before the true Christ was ever born**. No wonder the pagans did not accept Jesus Christ as the Son of God. They already worshipped a false son of god and his mother. Isn't it interesting that the *"mystery"* religion of Babylon is described as a *woman*? We know she represents a religion that is unfaithful to Christ, but could she also be a hint about the nature of Babylonian spirituality? The pseudo-Trinity of the Babylonians had a major difference from the true Trinity; **it included a female**.

MYSTERY RELIGION

Since the Babylonian worship was carried on through mysterious *"symbols,"* thus it was known as the *"mystery"* religion. In a similar way, the **occult** and **Satanism** has always **functioned in secret** or *"esoteric"* knowledge. Since Nimrod was believed to be the sun-god, **Baal-fire** was considered his earthly representation. Thus, **candles** and fires were **lighted in his honor**. He was also represented by sun symbols, fish, trees, pillars, and animals.

Interestingly, one of the Ten Commandments that the Lord gave Moses directly opposed such symbolism and imagery. Israel was not to **"... make unto thee any graven image, or any likeness of any thing that is in heaven above, or any thing that is in the earth beneath, or that is in the water under the earth ..."** (Ex. 20:4).

Another major symbol of Babylonian worship was the golden calf, which symbolized Tammuz, the son of the sun god. No wonder God was so angry with the children of Israel when Aaron fashioned for them a golden calf to worship. That golden calf was essentially a false Christ figure, another Jesus! *"They have turned aside quickly out of the way which I commanded them: they have made them a molten calf, and have worshipped it, and have sacrificed thereunto, and said, These be thy gods, O Israel, which have brought thee up out of the land of Egypt"* (Ex. 32:8).

It was later confirmed in the Book of Acts, among other Scriptural testimony, when Paul exhorted the Church that they **"... ought not to think that the Godhead is like unto gold, silver, or stone, graven by art and man's device"** (Acts 17:29). Paul condemned efforts to visibly represent the invisible God. God gives clear instruction and doctrine through the spoken and written Word.

Satan offers **mysterious** knowledge that is largely understood through the language of symbolism. With the destruction of the Tower of Babel, the Lord clearly showed His wrath against such a system of idolatry. *"Therefore is the name of it called Babel; because the LORD did there confound the language of all the earth: and from thence did the LORD scatter them abroad upon the face of all the earth"* (Gen.11:9). Even today, in one form or another, we find evidence of the mystery religion of Babylon in all false religions of the earth.

ROME

When Rome became a world empire, it naturally assimilated the pagan gods and religions from the countries over which it ruled into its own system of government and politics. To make matters worse, men began to set themselves up as *"lords"* over God's people, substituting their ideas and methods for God-given offices, gifts, and callings. Like Nimrod establishing a kingdom on earth, men in the Church tried to establish the Church as an earthly kingdom. This included the idea of Pontiff or Pontifex Maximus; essentially, this was the same office of the ancient Babylonian priest-king.

Therefore, Babylonian paganism, which had originally been carried out under the rulership of Nimrod, was united under the rulership of one man at Rome, Julius Caesar. It was the year, 63 B.C. that Julius Caesar was officially recognized as the *"Pontifex Maximus"* of the mystery religion — now re-established at Rome. It is well-known that this title and office continued to be held by each of the Roman emperors for many subsequent years.

It was during this time of Rome's world rule, with her previously established and accepted paganism, that the true Savior, Jesus Christ, was born and lived among men. After the Death and Resurrection of The Lord Jesus Christ, the Holy Spirit was sent by God to establish the New Testament Church on earth. Great signs and wonders were performed as God confirmed His Word. Anointed by the Holy Spirit, True Christianity swept the world. The early Christians turned the world upside down with their powerful message and Spirit — the pure Gospel of Jesus Christ. However, from the very beginning of this **true move of God**, Paul **warned the early Church** to **"earnestly contend for the faith."** *"Now the Spirit speaketh expressly, that in the latter times some shall depart from the faith, giving heed to seducing spirits, and doctrines of devils"* (I Tim. 4:1).

While the Early Church may have expected to defend against blatant paganism, the real danger would come in a much more deceptive way. Paganism, after the death of the Apostles and their students, began to gradually **blend** into the **Church's doctrine and practices**. This made the discernment a little more difficult, the paganism a little harder to recognize. While the New Testament was still being written, attempts were being made to corrupt Christian doctrine, so even the pure translation of the Bible was at stake in this regard. Jude warned that the counterfeit doctrines of the pagans were already beginning to work in the Church. *"Beloved when I gave all diligence to write unto you of the common salvation, it was needful for me to write unto you, and exhort you that ye should earnestly contend for the faith which was once delivered unto the saints. For there are certain men crept in unawares, who* *were before of old ordained to this condemnation, ungodly men, turning the grace of our God into lasciviousness, and denying the only Lord God, and our Lord Jesus Christ"* (Jude vss. 3-4).

CONSTANTINE

Church history shows that the majority of the marriage between Christianity and Paganism began with Constantine, the first and self-proclaimed Pope or *"Vicar of Christ"*. This proclamation in itself was a step back to the Babylonian mystery religion of symbols and images. Take, for example, the **second council of Nicea's** decree that ***"the image of God was as proper an object of worship as God Himself."*** The Pope was to be a symbol of Christ on earth with infallible authority. Constantine succeeded his father, Constantinus, when he died in A.D. 306.

Constantinus was a civil, caring, meek, gentle, and liberal man who desired to do good to all that were under his authority. It is said he had love and affection for the Word of God and guided his life and his rule by it. Because of this, he did not engage in wars that were contrary to his piety and Christian doctrine. Likewise, he refused to assist other leaders who were engaged in unjust wars. He stopped the destruction of Churches and commanded that Christians be preserved, defended, and kept safe from all injuries caused by persecution. He allowed Christians to practice their faith before him.

Though a benevolent ruler like his father before him, Constantine ruled with absolute power — oppressive and tyrannical. When Constantine first became emperor of the west, he faced many problems. Maxentieus was emperor of Rome. Maxentieus was a wicked ruler. He would fly into violent rages and then command his soldiers to kill large numbers of Roman citizens. He was addicted to the magical arts; he often called upon devils for help in his wickedness and sought wisdom from them. He was considered by many to be another Nero.

Weary of all the bloodshed, the citizens of Rome complained to Constantine. He listened and sympathized with them. He wrote a letter to Maxentieus and appealed to him to stop his corrupt actions and cruelty. When his letters did no good, he gathered his armies together in Britain and France and prepared to march on Rome in A.D. 313.

Constantine had also been concerned with the supposed **"magical powers"** of Maxentieus and wanted to make sure they would not prosper and overtake his rule. Being influenced by **"pagan superstition,"** Constantine looked toward heaven for a sign of help. It was the **"language of signs and wonders"** through which Constantine received his message to finally conquer Rome. On that evening Constantine saw a cross in the sky displaying the Greek words, *en toutor nika*, meaning, *"in this sign we conquer."* Then Constantine had a corresponding dream in which a voice commanded him to **mark his soldiers' shields with the "cross"** he had seen in his vision. This cross is pictured as the letter X with a line drawn through it and curled around the top. The night after he saw this **"vision,"** he said Christ appeared to him in a dream with the same **"cross,"** telling him that if he would make such a cross and carry it into his battles, he would always be victorious. Constantine had a cross **made of gold and precious stones** to carry in place of his standard, and he took over Rome successfully.

THE CROSS

Interestingly, the **"cross"** that Constantine saw closely resembled the Mithras **"cross of light"** that the followers of the **"sun god"** would accept because it was also one of their most sacred emblems. This way, **"the apostate Christians"** believed they were fighting for the Cross of Christ, and **"the pagans"** believed they were fighting for their **"cross of light."** The secret cult of Mithras worshiped Mithra, the light and power behind the sun. Mithra was called **"the divine Sun, the Unconquered Sun"** and was deemed **"the mediator"** between heaven and earth. The Mithras values reflected **prominent religious ideas** that **utilized astrology and magic**; it also included a **very unchristian ritual which attempted to bring about the ascent and immortalization of a man's soul**.

Actually, there is little reason to consider Constantine's vision authentic. The only authority from which historians gathered the story is from Eusebeies, who has been accused of being a *"falsifier of history."*

Regardless, if the vision was genuine, it **came from the spirit world of darkness** rather than the Lord. Jesus never told His disciples to kill others *"under a cross banner"* or give *"wicked rulers instructions to kill and fight as His representative."* However, **this** *"cross"* was the perfect symbol to bring agreement between what once were rightly *"opposing faiths."* **It gave** the two faiths a **reason** to look **for common ground**.

Constantine's worship of the sun god, while simultaneously professing Christianity, could be the result of such thinking. He used both pagan and Christian rites in the dedication of his new city, Constantinople. He even put an image of his own face on the statue of the sun god, and the city's currency included images of the sun.

Many *"apostate Christians"* followed his example and incorporated **sun worship** into their lives. Sunday (the day of the Roman sun god) was made into a day of rest. They celebrated the birth of Jesus on the day following the winter solstice, the day sun worshipers celebrated the birthday of the sun god (Dec.25). They prayed kneeling towards the east (where the sun rises) and believed that Jesus drove his chariot across the sky (from east to west). **Please remember** that **Nimrod** (a.k.a. Baal) was this ancient sun god of the universe, the one who had set up a kingdom *"against the Lord."* It is therefore not surprising to see that **more of his family** would appear in the Church — the **worship of the queen mother now called Mary**, the Blessed Virgin.

By and large, the **unifying symbol of a cross** in front of a sun helped to build a very powerful and unified Roman Empire. Any cross design used among various religions, societies, and organizations today still continue to carry significant symbolic meaning to its members.

THE STATE CHURCH

Constantine's goal was to have a state church where the church leaders functioned like members of a civil governing body, so **peace** *"among pagans and Christians"* was essential. The Bishop of Rome rose to political power and prestige; many considered Rome to be the most important city in the world. The Biblical office of elder/deacon was transformed into the office of the Catholic bishop, and bishops were the only ones who could become Popes. The Pope was elected as one bishop among brother bishops from numerous cities.

Constantine believed that the apostles were important mediators of salvation, and that he was on this same level. He even wanted his body to be kept in the Church of the Apostles **(an organized church he established)** along with the bodies of the other apostles. His coffin was to be in the middle with six apostles on each side of him. Doesn't this remind you of Christ and His twelve Disciples? It should since **Constantine** intended to be the *"Vicar of Christ"* on earth.

The kingdom *"against the Lord"* was escalating once again, but the *"union of church and state"* needed to be strongly established like it was under the early Babylonian priest-king of the mystery religion. This was largely solidified between Constantine and Bishop Silvester.

Bishop Silvester wanted to grow the church using Roman power including the Roman roads, Roman wealth, Roman law, and the Roman military. In the name of *"church growth,"* he chose to use the strengths and practical power of his sophisticated civilization to bring in the masses. In A.D. 313, Constantine, in his Edict of Milan, made Christianity the official religion of Rome, and subsequently approved Silvester as Bishop in A.D. 314.

Unlike relations between many prior bishops and emperors, Constantine treated Silvester like royalty. He *"confessed his sins"* to Silvester and took his advice. So-called *"Christians"* were no longer persecuted like the early apostles had been; they were now crowned as princes on earth — Silvester being the first Bishop to ever receive a physical crown. Constantine set the trend in a new direction; *"Christians"* were now **honored** as respected members of society. However, history shows that *"true Christians,"* such as Luther and Wycliffe, were still persecuted when they stood for the uncompromised Gospel.

A MIXTURE OF RELIGIOUS BELIEFS

The brotherhood of Constantine and Silvester was the first in a long line of alliances between the Roman Empire and the Church, and it marked the genuine birth of the Roman Catholic Church as we know it today — **a mixture of religious beliefs**, maintaining a strong influence on civil government and society. Constantine gained influence within both the offices of Pontifex Maximus (high priest of the mystery religion) and Pope (head of the Roman Catholic Church).

In A.D. 378, Demus, Bishop of Rome, was formally elected as *"Pontifex Maximus — official High Priest of the mysteries."* Amid the disordered and greedy power struggle of leadership at the time, historians have had some difficulty naming the first official Pope of the United Roman Catholic Church, meaning the combined Eastern and Western divisions of the church. With his *"Roman spirit of dominion,"* Leo I, known as Leo the Great, has been said to have been worthy of such status. At the death of his predecessor, Sixtus III, Leo I was elected Pope by a unified majority of clergy, senate, and citizens in A.D. 440. Leo claimed authority over the whole church, solely basing such authority on succession to the apostle Peter. However, it has also been said that Gregory I, in A.D. 590, truly ushered in the strict papacy as we know it today with full apostolic authority.

Still many, without hesitation, regard **Constantine** as the first Pope for his great success at uniting church and state. All accounts of Constantine indicate that he **was never truly born-again**. He committed several murders apart from those in battle, two of which were his wife and son. Everyone was forced to convert to his false version of *"Christianity,"* now the state religion, and he also continued to rely on pagan magical formulas to protect crops and heal disease. He had no problem holding the position of Pontifex Maximus even though others such as Emperor Gratin refused to be Pontifex Maximus. Emperor Gratin, *"for Christian reasons,"* believed that the title was **idolatrous** and **blasphemous**. Constantine, on the other hand, continually gave pagan practices a *"Christian veneer"* to help solicit support for the church.

Constantine did do some favors for the Christian faith such as abolishing death by crucifixion and stopping the brutal persecution of Christians in Rome. However, they were really self-serving. Constantine realized that persecution was not destroying the Christian faith, and he was actually in need of the Christian support because his position was being challenged by a rival emperor. Therefore, he needed a strong united front to his empire. **Instead of the empire being divided** — the *"pagans opposing the Christians"* — why not take the steps necessary to *"mix them together"* **under the banner of the cross? So clever was this mixture — the merging of paganism and Christianity — that one man was now revered by both pagans and professing Christians**. He was looked to by the *"church"* as bishop of bishops and by the *"pagans"* as the great interpreter of mysteries.

Attempting to make sure the discrepancy was covered, church leaders sought to find more similarities between the two religions. They knew that if they could find even a few points both sides had in common, they could merge them into one. By this time, the majority were not concerned with details. The great desire was for numbers and political power. Truth was secondary among such worldly-minded religious leaders.

Does this sound familiar? In their rush to *"combine the world and Christianity,"* it is exactly the same mind frame and reasoning as the **predominant church growth movements of today** — *Purpose Driven Life, Seeker-Sensitive, G-12*, etc.

CHAPTER TWO

PETER, THE FIRST POPE?

The newly organized sociopolitical *"church"* now found itself facing a vital how-to problem — that is, how to successfully merge paganism and Christianity. One man had to be looked upon by all as Head. He must be looked to by the *"church"* as *"bishop of bishops,"* while the pagans regarded him as their Pontifex Maximus. But, how could one man be both the head of the church and the head interpreter of the pagan mysteries at the same time? In an attempt to cover the discrepancy, church leaders sought for similarities between the two religions. They knew that if they could only find a few points in common, they could blend the two because the majority was not concerned with details. Their desire was for numbers, money, and political power. Concern for **"truth"** was secondary if considered a relevant issue at all.

The *"church"* did merge into paganism and accordingly, into apostasy as well. Somewhere the real Jesus Christ, the only true **mediator** between God and man, got lost in the mix. The *"church"* leaders would *"Christianize"* the pagan office of *"Pontifex Maximus"*, transforming him into the *"interpreter of Rome,"* the interpreter of the Roman Catholic Church. Astoundingly, yet perfectly demonstrating the customary occultic practice of wordplay, they found a tool for the trade: the actual word *"Peter,"* which we will discuss later.

ROMAN CATHOLIC TEACHING

Right now let's review the traditional, though outrageously mistaken, Roman Catholic teaching that the apostle Peter was the first Pope. According to Roman Catholic doctrine, Christ appointed Peter as the first Pope, who then went to Rome and served in that capacity for twenty-five years. Beginning with Peter, the Catholic Church claims a succession of Popes to this day, and upon this belief, the entire framework of Catholicism is built. But, does Scripture teach that Christ ordained *"one"* man to be above all others in His Church? Can we find any Scriptural authority for the office of Pope, a Supreme Pontiff? Did the early Christians recognize Peter as such?

The answer is *"no."* Scripture makes it plain that there was to be **equality** among the members of Christ's Church and that *"He," "is the Head of the Church,"* not the Pope (Eph. 5:23). If Roman Catholic doctrine was true, when James and John came to the Lord and asked if one of them could sit on His right hand and the other on His left hand, Jesus' answer would have been somewhat different. Christ would have undoubtedly given the right-hand place to Peter without a designation of left-hand positions.

JESUS' ANSWER TO PETER

Here is the answer Jesus actually gave: *"And James and John, the sons of Zebedee, come unto him, saying, Master, we would that thou shouldest do for us whatsoever we shall desire. And He said unto them, what would ye that I should do for you? They said unto Him, Grant unto us that we may sit, one on thy right hand, and the other on thy left hand, in thy glory. But Jesus said unto them, Ye know not what ye ask: can ye drink of the cup that I drink of? and be baptized with the baptism that I am baptized with? And they said unto Him, We can. And Jesus said unto them, ye shall indeed drink of the cup that I drink of; and with the baptism that I am baptized withal shall ye be baptized: But to sit on my right hand and on my left hand is not mine to give; but it shall be given to them for whom it is prepared. And when the ten heard it, they began to be much displeased with James and John. But Jesus called them to Him, and saith unto them, Ye know that they which are accounted to rule over the Gentiles exercise lordship over them; and their great ones exercise authority upon them. But so shall it not be among you: but whosoever will be great among you, shall be your minister"* (Mk. 10:35-43).

In these verses we find Jesus telling his disciples that they were not to act like kings, they were not to wear crowns, they were not to sit on thrones, and they were not to pattern themselves after heathen rulers. Yet every Pope has done these things down through the centuries. In these verses our Lord was plainly saying that none of the apostles were to set themselves up as rulers over others. Instead, the principles He taught clearly contradicted a **hierarchal church government** headed by a *"council of cardinals"* and a Pope having full **authority** as the *"bishop of bishops."* And before the Protestant Church forgets to *"remove the plank from their own eye,"* a *"leader of leaders,"* is the current Protestant version of such a chain of command.

*"For they bind heavy burdens and grievous to be borne, and lay them on men's shoulders; but they themselves will not move them with one of their fingers. But all their works they do for to be seen of men: they make broad their phylacteries, and enlarge the borders of their garments, and love the **uppermost rooms** at feasts and the **chief seats** in the synagogues, And greetings in the markets, and to be called of men, Rabbi, Rabbi. But be not ye called **Rabbi (meaning "teacher")**: for One is your **Master**, even Christ; and all ye are brethren. And call no man your **father** upon the earth: for One is your **Father**, which is in heaven. Neither be ye called masters: for One is your Master, even Christ"* (Mat. 23:4-10).

In this passage, Jesus even warned the disciples not to use flattering titles such as *"father"* (the word *"Pope"* means *"father"*), *"rabbi,"* or *"master."* *"For One is your Master, even Christ,"* He said, *"and all ye are brethren."* The idea of one of them being exalted to the position of the *"Holy Father"* (the Pope) is at utter variance with this text.

Ironically, many other organized societies and/or religions besides the Catholic Church take on such titles: the Shinto religion, the Confucian creed, Fraternal organizations, and Masonic/Secret orders to name a few. Something about that *"ladder of success"* and seemingly self-merited rank appeals to many. It is even glorified in the movies — the most outstanding example currently being the epic trilogy, *Star Wars*, where the characters are known as *"knights"*, *"masters"*, *"teachers"*, *"fathers"*, etc. who work diligently for **"global peace."** They hold **"high councils"** and draw their power from a spiritual **"force,"** never forgetting to state, *"may the force be with you"* at every critical departing. Apparently, real people like living this drama too. *"But in his estate (speaks of the Anti-Christ) shall he honor the **god of forces**: and a god whom his fathers knew not shall he honor with gold, and silver, and with **precious stones**, and pleasant things"* (Dan. 11:38).

WAS PETER SUPERIOR TO OTHERS?

The Roman Catholic teaching made Peter greatly superior to the other disciples. The main verse Catholics use to support this claim is *"And I say also unto thee, That thou art Peter, and upon this rock I will build my church; and the gates of hell shall not prevail against it"* (Mat. 16:18). If we take this verse in its proper setting, we can plainly see that the Church was not to be built on Peter, but on Christ.

In the verses just before, Jesus asked His disciples who men were saying that He was. *"When Jesus came into the coasts of Caesarea Philippi, He asked His disciples, saying, Whom do men say that I the Son of Man am. And they said, Some say that thou art John the Baptist: some, Elias; and others, Jeremias, or one of the prophets"* (Mat. 16:13-14). Then Jesus asked, *"He saith unto them, but whom say ye that I am?"* (Mat. 16:15). In verse 16, we find Peter answering the Lord's question, *"And Simon Peter answered and said, Thou art the Christ, the Son of the living God."* Although this proclamation is Peter speaking for all, it asserted a personal revelation as well, seeing that the Lord answered Peter directly in verse 17. Jesus then said, *"Thou art Peter, and upon this rock I will build my church."* Jesus was saying that Peter would now be called *"Cephas"* (Peter) and that the True Church would be founded and grounded on the solid, unchanging rock of truth that Jesus Christ is the One and Only Son of the Living God.

It was Peter's answer that Christ was acknowledging, not Peter's name. The Aramaic word that Christ used for *"Peter"* is *"Cephas,"* meaning *"a stone,"* a stone that may be thrown here or there. In the Greek, *"Cephas"* is *"Petros,"* denoting *"a piece of rock,"* not the same meaning for the term *"Rock"* in Christ's following words. In the phrase *". . . upon this Rock . . .,"* the word used for *"Rock"* is *"Petra,"* meaning *"a mass of Rock,"* *"a large Rock,"* a mighty immovable mass of Rock — the Godhead of Christ. *"And did all drink the same spiritual drink: for they drank of that spiritual **Rock** that followed them: and that **Rock** was **Christ**"* (I Cor. 10:4).

ROCK!

The word, *"Rock"* used by Christ in verse 17 described Himself just as the Lord has been described as a spiritual Foundation Rock or Stone throughout Scripture. *". . . The Lord is my **Rock**, and my fortress, and my deliverer"* (II Sam. 22:2). *". . . I will liken him unto a wise man, which built his house upon a **rock**: And the rain descended, and the floods came, and the winds blew, and beat upon that house; and it fell not: for it was founded upon a **rock**"* (Mat. 7:24-25). *"And he beheld them, and said, What is this then that is written, The **Stone** which the **Builders** rejected, the same is become the **Head of the corner**? Whosoever shall fall upon that **Stone** shall be broken; but on whomsoever it shall fall, it will grind him to powder"* (Lk. 20:17-18).

These all speak of the Lord Jesus Christ or some aspect of the true Godhead. Referring to Christ as the **"Head Corner Stone"** really puts things into perspective. Clearly, Peter is neither the head nor foundation of the Church. Jesus is the **Chief Corner Stone**, the **Foundation Rock** that is in the highest place of honor and usefulness. Jesus is the spiritual cement and primary support, the Rock that literally holds the Church together! Jesus must be placed first for the work to be complete; He is the Author and Finisher of the true faith!

WHO IS THE BUILDER?

The **"Builders"** in Luke 20:17 were Jewish *"wise men"* — the

18 *The Modern Babylon*

elders, priests, and scribes of Israel. They called themselves *"builders"* because they practiced *"the building of the world"* which is also *"the law."* However, these *"builders"* rejected Jesus as the Rock, just as the Roman Catholic Church rejects Jesus as the Rock today.

Rather, the *"chief cornerstone"* of the Roman Catholic Church is Peter, the man they claim was the first Pope, a modern *"world-builder"* and keeper of tradition. In fact, *"Pontifex"* in Latin means **"bridge-builder,"** signifying the bridge between man and God. Perhaps those who want to be labeled as *"builders"* in the present organizational church world — *"kingdom-builders," "consensus-builders,"* and/or *"bridge-builders,"* (not to mention the illusive underground *"builders"* called *"masons"*) — should take great care that they, too, do not fulfill the prophecy and reject the same Stone.

Curiously, a major **archetypal** character of the Tarot (major instrument of divination) has long been the Hierophant, also known as the Holy See or *"one who shows;"* he was *"the speaker of the sacred mysteries"* and *"keeper of the **stories**."* Also, comic book writers who come up with false worlds of **myth** and enthrone super heroes like to be called *"world-builders."* The ancient Greeks called one with super-human or **god-like** abilities a *"hero." "They will turn their ears away from the truth and turn aside to **myths**"* (II Tim. 4:4). Man-made tradition or explanations for the world are myth rather than Truth.

The phrase *"thou art Peter"* is actually the fulfillment of Peter's promised name change given to him in John 1:41-42: *"He first findeth his own brother Simon, and saith unto him, We have found the Messias, which is, being interpreted, the Christ. And he brought him to Jesus. And when Jesus beheld him, he said, Thou art Simon the son of Jona: thou shalt be called Cephas."*

In Biblical culture, a name did more than identify; it communicated something of essence, the character or the reputation of the person or thing named. Names were, at times, changed by the Lord. For example, Abram's name meaning *"exalted father,"* was changed to Abraham meaning *"father of the multitudes."* When Jesus said, *"Thou shalt be called Cephas,"* rather than *". . . Simon, the son of Jona . . ."* He illustrated His ability to change men fundamentally and characteristically, to recreate men.

Even though Jesus promised Peter a new name which proclaimed what the Holy Spirit would make of him, as we study the Gospels, we find that he did not take on the new name until he was deserving of it. Jesus never actually called him anything but Simon until the appointed time (Mat. 17:25; Mk. 14:37; Lk. 22:31; Jn. 21:15-17). Jesus officially bestowed Peter's new name upon his **confession of the True Faith**, the Faith that confesses **Jesus as The Christ** no matter what others may say (Mat. 16:16-17). Peter was clarifying his Faith. Jesus Christ is more than just a man! Jesus Christ is the Messiah and Savior, and this confession is what earned Peter a new name! A new name! Likewise, this same confession today bestows a new name to a repentant sinner who is saved by Faith in the Precious Blood of Jesus Christ, and that new name is written in the Lamb's Book of Life.

PETER IN ROME?

In order to aid the merge of Christianity and paganism and try to prove that Peter was the first Pope, it was necessary to teach that the apostle Peter had gone to Rome. However, there is not a shred of evidence that Peter was ever in Rome.

The Roman Catholic Church claims that Peter went to Rome in about A.D. 41 and was martyred there in about A.D. 66. The New Testament, on the other hand, tells us that Peter went to Antioch, to Samaria, to Goppa, to Caesarea, and other places, but it never mentions Rome! This would be a strange omission since Rome was the Empire's capitol and considered the most important city in the world!

Nevertheless, Roman Catholic tradition claims that Peter suffered martyrdom there after a Pontificate of twenty-five years. If we accept A.D. 66 as the date of his martyrdom, it would mean that he was bishop of Rome from A.D. 41 to A.D. 66. But, the Bible tells us that he was at the Council at Jerusalem around A.D. 44 (Acts Chpt. 15). In about A.D. 53, Paul was with him in Antioch, *"But when Peter was come to Antioch, I withstood him to the face, because he was to be blamed."* (Gal. 2:11) In approximately A.D. 58, Paul wrote his letter to the Christians in Rome in which he sent greetings to twenty-seven persons; notably these letters never greeted or even mentioned Peter. Can you imagine a missionary writing a letter to a Church and greeting twenty-seven of the most prominent members of the Church without greeting the Pastor? Remember, these letters were the way the apostles communicated to the entirety of the Church and therefore, read to the whole body of Believers.

THE MAN PETER

Let's go on to compare Peter with other Popes. It soon becomes apparent that Peter's activity in the Church was completely different from that of a Pope:

1. The fact that Peter was a married man does not harmonize well with the strict Catholic position that the Pope is to be unmarried. Scripture tells us that Peter's mother-in-law was healed of a fever. *"But Simon's wife's mother lay sick of a fever, and anon they tell him of her"* (Mk. 1:30). *"And when Jesus was come into Peter's house, he saw his wife's mother laid, and sick of a fever"* (Mat. 8:14). Some try to explain this discrepancy by saying that Peter ceased to live with his wife. Did she leave him? Did he leave her? If he did, he was a wife-deserter. In either case, Peter would be a poor foundation upon which to build a Church. The Bible plainly shows that Peter did not leave his wife. Twenty-five years after Jesus ascended to heaven, the apostle Paul mentioned that the various apostles had wives — including Cephas, the Aramaic name for Peter. *"Have we not power to lead about a sister, a wife, as well as other apostles, and as*

the brethren of the Lord, and Cephas?" (I Cor. 9:5) So, it is obvious Peter had not left his wife.

TRADITION?

2. Popes place tradition in a place of equal importance to the Word of God. Peter, however, had little faith in customs of men. *"Forasmuch as ye know that ye were not redeemed with corruptible things, as silver and gold, from your vain conversation received by tradition from your fathers"* (I Pet. 1:18). Peter's sermon on the day of Pentecost was filled with the Word of God, not the tradition of men. When the people asked what they should do to get right with God, Peter did not tell them to have a little water sprinkled or poured on them. Instead he said, *". . . Repent, and be baptized every one of you in the name of Jesus Christ for the remission of sins, and ye shall receive the gift of the Holy Ghost"* (Acts 2:38). Repentance is the answer; baptism is only an outward testimony of the repentance.

WORSHIP?

3. Peter would not allow people to bow down to him. *"And as Peter was coming in, Cornelius met him, and fell down at his feet, and worshipped him. But Peter took him up, saying, Stand up; I myself also am a man"* (Acts 10:25-26). This is quite different from what a Pope would have said. Men routinely bow to the Pope and kiss his ring, and he loves to have them do so. Especially devout Catholics even bow to statues of the Pope. *"Thou shalt not **bow** down thyself to them, nor serve them: for I the LORD thy God am a jealous God . . ."* (Ex. 20:5).

CROWNS?

4. Peter wore no crowns. Peter taught that God's people were not to wear crowns in this life; the only crown Jesus Himself wore while on earth was a crown of thorns. Do

> we deserve better than our Lord? *"The disciple is not above his master: but every one that is perfect shall be as his master"* (Lk. 6:40). However Peter explained that, *"when the Chief Shepherd shall appear, you shall receive a crown of glory that fadeth not away"* (I Pet. 5:4). *". . . Now they do it to obtain a corruptible crown; but we an incorruptible"* (I Cor. 9:25).

The truth is Peter never acted like a Pope, never dressed like a Pope, and never spoke like a Pope. People never approached him as a Pope because Peter was not a Pope. Again and again, the claims of the Roman Catholic Church regarding Peter as the first Pope and apostolic succession residing in the Bishop of the Catholic Church are abrogated. It is a lie devised by men through the twisting of Scripture to promote their doctrine.

The True Church of Jesus Christ has Christ as its Head and is, therefore, a spiritual organism. The Catholic Church is purely a human organization, and as a result, has no proper spirituality at all. Humans never have been and never will be God; Jesus Christ has always been and always will be God.

As well, many other cases expose the error claiming Peter was the first Pope. It was not until the time of Calixtus (bishop in Rome from A.D. 218-A.D. 223), that the Scripture, Matthew 16:18, was first used in an attempt to prove that the bishop of Rome was Peter's succession. The phrase, *"I will build My church"* speaks as well of the Church belonging to Christ, and thereby headed up by Christ, not Peter or any other man. In Matthew 18:1, the disciples asked Jesus to tell them who was the greatest in the kingdom. *"At the same time came the disciples unto Jesus, saying, Who is the greatest in the kingdom of heaven?"* If Jesus had, in fact, said Peter was the one upon whom the Church was to be built and to become Pope, then the disciples would have already known who was the greatest among them.

CHAPTER THREE

We will now return to the actual word *"Peter,"* for this has become the occult's greatest play-on-words to date. The Hebrew Lexicon explains that the consonantal word (word without vowels) in the original Hebrew language for *"Peter"* was **"P-T-R,"** meaning *"to interpret,"* and had always related to oracle interpretation. Spellings vary since vowels are changeable between languages, especially in the Semitic language. In the ancient mystery religions the chief pagan **gods**, the pagan **priests**, and the pagan **temples** were **all** called **"*PeTeRs.*"** This was the key to connecting the office of Pontifex Maximus to the office of Pope; the Pontifex Maximus was called *"Peter"* and the first Pope was allegedly Peter the apostle.

The pagan priests called *"Peters"* had superior **knowledge**, both **spiritually** and **intellectually**. The Lord has forbidden such knowledge since the Garden of Eden. See, the unauthorized **esoteric knowledge** of the occult has always been, not so much a matter of becoming the one and only God as much as it is a matter of **"*becoming like god.*"** To make matters worse, the term *"Peter"* or *"Pator"* had also taken on the more secular meaning of *"parent"* or *"father."* Fathers were also known as *"Archpators"* or *"Patriarchs."* This came about largely since the father was considered the chief priest of the family in ancient cultures. Thus, to the blinded *"Christians"* of the apostasy, the *"Pope"* or *"Holy Father"* was the succession of Peter the apostle while, to the integrated pagans, he was the succession of the chief/father *"Peter-gods"*.

PETER

The deep-rooted name for the divine interpreters, the *"Peters,"* lasted as late as Greek and Roman times. The chief Roman gods: Neptune, Saturn, Janus, Quirnus, and others were called *"Peters"*.

The chief, *"Father-god"*, Jupiter, actually had *"Peter"* incorporated in part of his name as *"Ju-Peter"*. The chief god of the Greeks was named Zeus, and *"Ju-Peter"* was the Roman way of saying *"Zeus-Peter"*. It has even been reported that the bronze statue of St. Peter sitting in his chair (located in St. Peter's Basilica) was originally a statue of Jupiter taken from the Pantheon (ancient pagan temple of the Romans). Also, the Greek god, Apollo, was called *"Patrius"*. The Thessalians likely worshipped Neptune under the name *"Poseidon Petraios"*. The chief instrument or idol used by the Ammonian priests in Egypt was labeled, *"Pietaurum,"* and the pagan gods are often pictured standing by stone pillars called *"Patroas"* or *"Peters"*.

These pillars became known as *"Peter-stones"* and are widespread throughout the history of the ancient world. The term *"Petra"* came to mean any large stone, but it originally always referred to the sacred *"Peter-stones"*. There is some legend about a stone or the word, *"Petra,"* in accounts of every major oracular temple. Again, we see who is really the chief corner stone in the Roman Catholic Church — the **chief Peter-stone**. Contemporary examples of such *"Peter-stones"* are called *"obelisks"*, some of the most disgraceful being the Washington Monument and one in the center of St. Peter's Square in Rome.

BALAAM

Furthermore, Balaam, had been called *"Pethor of Mesopotamia"* or *"Peter of Mesopotamia"*. Remember, Mesopotamia was the birthplace of false religion — the worship of the **sun** god, Nimrod. A *"Pethor"* also referred to a sacred **high place** of oracle interpretation where a **"college of priests"** appointed Balaam as the chief *"Patora"*. Not surprisingly, then, the meaning of the name *"Balaam"* in the Semitic language is the same as the meaning for *"Nimrod," (conqueror of the people)*. *"Nicolaus,"* was the Greek name for *"Nimrod,"* and also meant *"conqueror of the people."* Balaam was, thereby, the successor of Nimrod, the Pontifex Maxumus of the pagan world. The New Testament even speaks of the

Nicolaitanes who followed the teachings of Balaam. *"Yet I have left me seven thousand in Israel, all the knees which have not **bowed** unto **Baal**, and every mouth which hath not kissed him"* (I Ki. 19:18). Balaam's headquarters was *"Peter on the Euphrates"* or *"Saint Peter's of Mesopotamia."*

As power passed from one rising Empire to the next, the mystery religion of Babylon made its way from Mesopotamia to **Rome**, so Rome became the chief oracle of the world. Interestingly, St. Peter's Basilica today is considered one of the most holy places to Catholics; it supposedly hosts the tomb of St. Peter directly under the main altar. Apparently, the legendary motto, **"all roads lead to Rome,"** is experiencing a long-awaited spiritual resurrection. *"But take heed to yourselves: for they shall deliver you up to **councils**; and in the **synagogues** ye shall be beaten: and ye shall be brought before **rulers** and **kings** for my sake, for a **testimony** against them"* (Mk. 13:9).

NIMROD

Nimrod was actually known by another significant name — *"Mithras."* Mithras was the Persian name for the sun-god, Baal. Keep in mind that the Mithras *"cross of light"* which resembled Constantine's *"cross"* was used to combine the church and paganism. His temples were called *"Patra"* and *"Petra,"* his festivals were called *"Patrica,"* and he, himself, was called *"Pator"* by the nations of the East. Therefore, the cult of Mithras practiced blatant *"Peter-worship."* The implications of such are quite alarming!

The worship of the **sun** god, under the name *"Peter"* came right into the Roman Catholic Church and never left! Even the *"Peter-stone pillars"* were said to represent rays from the sun. Occultists believed that the spirit of the ancient Egyptian sun-god, Ra, resided in the modern day *"obelisk,"* so an obelisk actually represents the very presence of the **sun-god**. In fact, the obelisk in St. Peter's square in Rome is positioned so that every Pope must face it when they address the crowd. The ancient Egyptians believed that the **"sun"** was the **"eye"** of God, and occultists have long believed that spiritual knowledge and/or guidance comes from the East, the same direction from which the sun rises. *". . . His (Osiris) power was symbolized by an eye over the Scepter. The Sun was termed by the Greeks the Eye of Jupiter, and the Eye of the world; and his (The Sun glyph) is the All-Seeing Eye in our Lodges"* (Albert Pike, Morals and Dogma of the Ancient and Accepted Scottish Rite of Freemasonry, pp. 15-16, 477).

It should not be a shock, then, that *"Lucifer"* means *"light-bringer."* Man, under the lordship of the prince of this world (otherwise known as Satan or Lucifer), would logically worship the sun since it gives light. It is the greatest source of **light**, of **energy**, and seemingly of **power** in the universe. *"And no marvel; for Satan himself is transformed into an **angel of light**"* (II Cor. 11:14).

But all those who worship the sun are fair-warned; Revelation 21:23 tells us that Heaven does not need the light of the created sun or the moon: *"And the city had no need of the **sun**, neither of the **moon**, to shine in it: for the Glory of God did lighten it, and the Lamb is the **light** thereof."* The Lamb of God, Jesus Christ, is the True Light, the Light that will never cease.

On the other hand, there will be a time that, *"Yea, the **light** of the wicked shall be put out, and the spark of his fire shall not shine"* (Job 18:5). *". . . The **sun** shall be darkened, and the **moon** shall not give her light . . ."* (Mk. 13:24) In fact, Jesus warned us to make sure that what we think is **light** is not really **dark**: *"Take heed therefore that the light which is in thee be not darkness"* (Lk. 11:35).

THE TRUE POSITION OF PETER

Of course, it is undeniable that in the early days of the church the Apostle Peter did take a very prominent position among the Apostles. It was Peter who preached the first sermon after the Holy Spirit came at Pentecost, resulting in the Salvation of 3,000 souls in a single day. Peter was also the one who first took the Gospel to the Gentiles, but none of his works, by any stretch of the imagination, indicated that he took on the role of Pope or Universal Bishop and Bishops!

In fact, while Peter did seem to take the most outstanding role in the very beginning, Paul had the most outstanding ministry overall. Paul wrote 100 chapters with 2,325 verses in the New Testament, while Peter only wrote eight chapters with 166 verses. In Galatians 2:9, Paul spoke of Peter, James, and John as pillars in the Christian church. Yet Paul would say *". . . in nothing am I behind the very Chiefest Apostles, though I be nothing,"* emphasizing that, while he commends these men of God, none are greater than the others, and furthermore, none did anything for God in his own strength (II Cor. 12:11).

Galatians 2:11 is enough evidence alone to prove that Peter had no **apostolic authority** over the others. In this verse Paul had to rebuke Peter, *"But when Peter was come to Antioch, I withstood him to the face, because he was to be blamed."* Paul had to correct him, and Peter, in **humility**, heeded the exhortation.

Clearly, neither Peter nor any other man is an *"infallible"* Pope. Again, the Protestant church is not blameless in this regard. The **G-12 apostleship** misapplies Scripture as it decrees that the layman is not to *"touch God's anointed,"* and, as well, they claim that Christ granted denominational heads authority over local pastors. In a secular sense, the ease in which the industrialized nations of the **G-8** are bringing the world under its subjection with the help of *"faith-based"* programs would put the work of Adolph Hitler to shame. Not all who worship false gods do so simply because they choose to; many times it is enforced by law.

PAUL

What's more, Paul was considered to be *"the great apostle to the Gentiles."* *"For I speak to you Gentiles, inasmuch as I am the Apostle of the Gentiles, I magnify mine office"* (Rom. 11:13). Peter's ministry was *"unto the circumcision,"* the Jews. *"But contrariwise, when they saw that the Gospel of the uncircumcision was committed unto me, as the Gospel of the Circumcision was unto Peter; For He that wrought effectually in Peter to the Apostleship of the Circumcision, the same was mighty in me toward the Gentiles"* (Gal. 2:7-8).

Rome was a Gentile city, so it wouldn't have made any sense, according to Scripture, for Peter to be the Bishop of Rome. Obviously, these verses are not meant to imply that Paul was only to preach to the Gentiles and Peter was only to preach to the Jews; it meant that it was the main business of Paul to preach to the Gentiles and the main business of Peter to preach to the Jews. In other words, each group was primarily rather than exclusively entrusted to one of the two Apostles.

Some exceptions include that the Great Commission of preaching to the Gentiles was given first to Peter, that Peter preached the first message to a Gentile (Acts, Chpt. 10), and that Paul often preached in the Synagogues of the Jews. Also, the earliest churches were mixed bodies (both Jews and Gentiles), exactly as they should have been. Both Peter and Paul preached in these churches.

Today, a genuine congregation of Jesus Christ will be mixed as well — black and white, old and young, rich and poor, educated and uneducated. If your church makes an easy **target market**, watch out! *"For there is no respect of persons with God"* (Rom. 2:11).

THE LIE

Apparently a **lie** can be so huge people actually refuse to believe it is a lie. Call it pride, fear, distaste for change — whatever, but chosen delusion is a serious problem.

The Papacy and, even more specifically, that the Papacy began with Peter is a great lie, and it has been accepted for so long that piles of fictitious evidence have been collected to support it. Now, to many, it seems more unbelievable to think it could be a lie than to think that a lie of this magnitude has been allowed to continue at all. In fact, many have a hard time believing both secular and Biblical evidence to the contrary. They may even consider it audacious or sacrilegious to think that something so well-established, especially in the name of God, could be untrue. Satanists actually figured out this phenomenon ages ago; they count on the concept of *"audacity"* to cover their wicked deeds. *"And for this cause God shall send them strong delusion, that they should **believe a lie**: That they all might be damned who believed not the Truth, but had pleasure in unrighteousness"* (II Thess. 2:11-12). God help us not to believe a lie!

God help us not to believe a lie even if our entire life has been built upon it, even if the lie is the only certainty we've ever known! If God has not already sent a strong delusion, help us to swallow our pride and prefer the Truth. This life is temporary; the next life is forever! *"Your terribleness has **deceived** you, and the **pride** of your heart, O thou who dwells in the clefts of the rock, who holds the height of the hill: though you should make your nest as high as the eagle, I will bring you down from thence, saith the LORD"* (Jer. 49:16).

A study of the Scriptures reveals that the Papal office was not instituted by Christ, the origin of the Papal office was that of man and, thereby, pagan in nature. The Papal/pagan church continued to search for more similarities that would further their lie and connect Peter with Rome.

For almost a thousand years before, the people of Rome had believed in the mystic *"keys"* — the sacred keys of the pagan god, Janus, and goddess, Cybele. According to tradition, Janus brought men from savagery to sophistication and was the first to build cities and establish government. Yes, Janus was just another name for the sun-god, Nimrod, who led the first organized rebellion on Earth by building Babylon, a city *"against the Lord."*

Janus was pictured with two faces, one face was young in appearance and the other was old (the older face signifying a later version of Nimrod incarnated in Tammuz). Janus was, therefore, the Babylonian Messiah as well. Besides his **reincarnation**, some have said the double-face also symbolized his sacred task of ***"civilizing"*** men, **transforming** them from one state to another state. This act in reality brought men from a state he could not control into a state he could control; he brought them into the *"state"* of Babylon — a task that continues through the Papacy and its *"papal-states"* to this very day.

A FALSE MESSIAH OF GOOD WORKS

The True Messiah brings true **morality** by changing the heart of man. False messiahs bring false morality by changing society. When a **civilization** is controlled by *"the moral majority"* it should take care that it has not traded the True Messiah for a false messiah of **good works**. *"For if Abraham were justified by **works**, he hath whereof to glory; but not before God"* (Rom. 4:2). The *"best-citizen"* award will not save you, and you could be the best citizen on Earth without being a citizen of Heaven at all. False religions are actually made up of false moral codes; false religion really could not exist without them.

One more note on the two-faced representation of Janus: The past and future was always on his mind; he interpreted the times and calendar, hence the first month of the year being titled JANUary. He could look forward and backward into time — in a sense, prophecy or predict the future. The very word *"Vatican"* means *"prophecy"* or divine knowledge. The Pope is, therefore, a modern-day Janus, the leading medium or seer in a location theoretically designated for *"holy"* foresight.

THE KEYS

The *"keys"* of Janus had been symbolic keys of the Mystery religion since olden times and have been found in various other forms and places. The Brahmatma, the Supreme Pontiff of India, was regarded as the preserver of the *"keys,"* bearing upon his tiara two crossed keys. Mithras carried two keys as symbols of his authority. The Turkish *"interpreters"* of the Koran were called, *"Mufties"*, and derive that name from the very same verb as that from which comes *"Miftah"*, a key. Thus, when the emperor claimed to be the successor of the *"gods,"* the Supreme Pontiffs of the Mysteries, the *"keys"* came to be a symbol of their authority also. When the Pope became the Pontifex Maximus in about A.D. 378, he automatically became the possessor of the Mystic *"keys."* This gained recognition for the Pope from the pagans, but how would this be associated with Christianity?

Again, the apostate church leaders saw an opportunity to mix Peter into the story. Janus was another ancient Roman god with the title, *"Peter."* The *"Peter-god,"* Janus, was called, *"keeper of the gates of Heaven and Earth"* and carried a key in his hand. The apostate church mixed the *"keys"* and Peter by taking what Christ had said to Peter in Matthew 16:19: *"And I will give unto thee the keys of the Kingdom of Heaven...."* It was not until A.D. 631, though, that the Pope publicly claimed that the keys he displayed as insignia of his spiritual authority were the keys that Christ gave to the Apostle Peter. This was over fifty years after the Pope had become the *"Pontifex Maximums,"* possessor of the *"keys."* It is evident, then, that these *"keys"* of Peter are the mystic keys of paganism, not *"keys"* given by Christ.

This passage of Scripture is misunderstood anyway. The *"keys"* the Lord gave to Peter were not literal keys. The key that was given to Peter and all the rest of the Disciples that the Lord sent forth was the message of the Gospel. Through the preaching of the pure Gospel of Jesus Christ, men could be saved and become part of the glorious Kingdom of God.

In their misinterpretation, many actually view Peter as the *"gate-keeper"* in which Peter decides who to let in and who to keep out of Heaven, perfectly demonstrating the ultimate **hypocrisy** of any religious system of law. No man determines Salvation. *"And no man in Heaven, nor in earth, neither under the earth, was able to open the Book, neither to look thereon"* (Rev. 5:3). Granting entrance into Heaven is the Lord's position only, and it exemplifies the greater plan of **Grace** that comes through **Faith** in Christ Jesus. It is only the faithful bride of Christ (the true invisible church) who will enter Heaven's *"pearly gates."* *"And while they went to buy, the bridegroom [Christ] came; and they who were ready went in with him to the marriage: and the door was shut"* (Mat. 25:10). Unfortunately, Peter's (the Pope's) faithful bride will enter through a very different set of gates.

GATE-KEEPER

Not surprisingly, however, the concept of Peter as the *"gate-keeper"* did line up to the **mythological** ideas of the pagans which placed Janus as the *"possessor of the keys"* and *"keeper of the doors, gates, and highways"* of Rome. The name, Janus, actually means *"gates."* Ovid's <u>Fasti</u> tells us that Janus' dual faces indicated his equal domain over both the heavens and the Earth and that all things could be open and shut at his will. He was called Patulclus or Clusius, *"the opener and the shutter."* This is absolute blasphemy! *"But woe unto you, Scribes and Pharisees, **hypocrites!** for ye shut up the Kingdom of Heaven against men: for ye neither go in yourselves, neither suffer ye them that are entering to go in"* (Mat. 23:13). Janus was actually the *"god of doors and hinges"*, and it was said that he had *"jus vertendi cardinis"* — the *"power of turning the hinge."* Therefore, he had the power of opening and shutting the doors of Heaven, and the power of opening and shutting the gates of **peace** and **war** on Earth. In effect, Janus was the great Mediator, worshipped as having all power in Heaven and Earth including governmental authority.

The term *"cardinal"* means *"hinge,"* so it is easy to see how the church's government, originally known as the Pope's Grand Council of State, came to be called the *"college of cardinals"* that is headed by the Pope, a descendant of Janus who could *"turn the hinge."* This is the unmistakable model of the *"Pagan College of Pontiffs"* and its *"Pontifex Maximus"* from the *"Grand Original Council of Pontiffs"* in Babylon.

THE COCK

To take this a little farther, not only were the *"keys"* a symbol of Janus, but the *"cock,"* a bird *"sacred"* to Janus, also represented him. The cock was a symbol of Mithra as well. In fact, many pagan religions that **worship** the **sun** also reverence the cock because the cock (or rooster) crows at sunrise. It heralds the sun!

In Greek mythology, Alectryon was given the mandate to guard Ares' door. When Alectryon failed to warn Ares (the god of war) that Helios (the sun) was going to enter, Ares turned Alectryon into a cock since they never fail to announce the arrival of the sun.

This is particularly interesting to see that this Greek character was given a position as the guardian of a door and then as an announcer of the sun. As we have seen, Popes supposedly guard the doors of Heaven and announce the Will of Christ, the Son of God. The problem is this particular Christ is looking more like the sun than the Son! Will this symbolic rooster (the Pope) herald the coming of the sun-god? Will the people think it is the real God? Just as the *"keys"* of Janus were associated with Peter, the *"sacred cock"* was associated with occurrences in Peter's life. Didn't a cock crow on the night that Peter denied the Lord? *"Peter then denied again: and immediately the cock crew"* (Jn. 18:27). So here was yet another connection — although a vague one — that was used to harmonize the pagan office of Pontifex Maximus (a.k.a. High Priest of Janus) with the office of Peter.

CHAPTER FOUR

In addition to this conclusive evidence, there is much more proof that the Pope is not the successor of the Apostle Peter, but is instead, the successor of the line of the High Priests of paganism — paganism that originated in Babylon. The very expensive and highly decorated garments that the Popes have worn confirm that the office of the Pope is of pagan origin, for such garments are patterned after those of the venerated Roman emperors, not the Apostles.

Historians have not let this fact go unnoticed; their testimony is that *"the vestments of the clergy were legacies from pagan Rome"* (*The Story of Civilization*, Vol. 4 p. 745). These deductions are common knowledge to students of religious study. Can you imagine the Apostles dressed like Popes? Of course not! The Apostles did not need to hide their beliefs with symbolic insignia; despite persecution, they proclaimed their Message loud and clear! Paul said: *"For I am **not ashamed** of the Gospel of Christ: for it is the Power of God unto Salvation . . ."* (Rom. 1:16).

THE TIARA

The tiara or *"triregnum"* that the Popes wear — though decorated in different ways at different times — is identical in shape to that worn by the *"gods"* or *"angels"* that are shown on ancient pagan Assyrian tablets and artifacts. It is the cap of the *"Magna Mater"*, the great nature goddess of ancient Phrygia in Asia Minor (a.k.a. The Great Mother, Cybele, or Semiramis). It is the tiara of Brahmatma (Supreme Pontiff of India) and resembles the tiara of the perpetually **reincarnating** Dalai Lama, the **god** and **ruler** of Tibet.

This crown is actually a triple crown (three tiaras) stacked in the shape of a **beehive** with a silver central core. Interestingly, the

36 *The Modern Babylon*

beehive is a prominent symbol of freemasonry. The *"Monitor"*, a masonic textbook, calls the **beehive** a *"hieroglyphical emblem"* of the order. This pertains to the ancient Egyptian pictorial writings called *"hieroglyphics,"* which, in Greek, means *"sacred carvings"* or *"words of the god."* Each tiara of the Pope's crown is heavily adorned with **golden decorations**, **enamel**, **diamonds**, **emeralds**, and other **jewels** and **precious stones**. Sometimes the decorations included forms of **crosses**, **leaves**, or **clovers**, and most are topped with a **crucifix**.

In 1805, in Milan's cathedral, Napoleon was crowned king of Italy with the *"Iron Crown of Lombardy,"* an ancient royal insignia of Europe. *"The Iron Crown"* gets its name from the narrow band of iron within it said to be made of the nails of crucifixion of Christ. Its outer circlet of the crown is made of **six gold** and **enamel** segments of beaten gold, joined together by hinges and set with **precious stones** that stand out in relief, in the form of **crosses** and **flowers**, amazingly similar to the traditional crowns of the Popes.

It is scary that these crowns are worn by both governmental dictators and *"infallible"* religious leaders and that the leader is most often the combined head of the religion and the state, just like the ancient Babylonian **Priest-Kings!** The most famous occasion when the triple tiara is used is the six-hour ceremony of the Papal Coronation when the new Pope is crowned with the words: *"Receive the tiara adorned with* **three crowns** *and know that thou art* **Father** *of princes and kings,* **Ruler** *of the world,* **Vicar** *of our Saviour Jesus Christ."* The True God of the Bible is described as a **Thrice-Holy God**. Such bold mockery will be judged by the Lord.

DAGON

The mitre worn by the Popes (and sometimes by Cardinals and Bishops) has an even more atrocious origin, an origin that provides us with another clue in solving the identity of today's modern Babylon and the true origin of the Papal office. It has been favored above the triple crown by recent Popes, but the *"triregnum"* has by no means been discarded.

The mitre worn by the Pope is actually the mitre of Dagon, the **fish-god**. As the noted writer, Hislop, puts it: *"The two-horned mitre, which the Pope wears when he sits on the high altar at Rome and receives the **adoration** of the **Cardinals** is the very mitre worn by Dagon, the fish-god of the Philistines and Babylonians. Students of Scripture know how hated this pagan worship of Dagon was in the sight of God."*

The god, Dagon, first appears in existing records dating about 2500 B.C. *"Dag"* meant *"fish"* and, therefore, represented the *"fish-god."* Old monuments of Dagon show him represented as half man and half fish (I Sam., Chpt. 5). Dagon was also pictured on Mesopotamian (Babylonian) sculptures. Though it originated in the paganism of Babylon, Dagon worship become popular among the Philistines. This is foreseeable for the Philistines because they lived in a coastal area. *"Then the lords of the Philistines gathered them together for to offer a great sacrifice unto Dagon their god, and to rejoice: for they said, Our god hath delivered Samson our enemy into our hand"* (Judg. 16:23).

The head of the fish formed a mitre above that of the man, while a scaly, fan-like tail fell as a cloak behind him, leaving the human limbs and feet exposed. We see here the use of the divided and somewhat pointed, fish-head mitre, looking as though the jaws of the fish were slightly opened. The fish-body was later removed, so eventually, only the fish-head adorned the great mediatorial god. On several Maltese pagan coins, this god (with characteristics similar to Osiris, the Egyptian Nimrod) is shown without the fish-body, just the fish-head mitre. The Chaldean priests of Babylon were described as wearing headgear like a fish's head. It is clearly the same type of pagan mitre that the Pope — the **Pontiff of Modern Babylon** — wears to this day!

THE FISH MEN

The Talmud, a heretical record of rabbinical discussion and ancient oral tradition, called *"Dag,"* the *"Messiah."* He is even identified with Matsya, the fish **avatar** of Krishna. Remember that the false "*Savior*" of Babylon in the "*Mysteries*" was represented in various ways and symbols. One of his **mystery forms** was a **fish**.

This false god eerily takes on different forms, physically and spiritually — **mutating** like a superhero, **reincarnating** its life-force, and/or **evolving** from a fish to a man to a god. Such evasion has made this slippery fish difficult to catch!

He even posed under the names Annedotus and Berosso as the creator of the Babylonian **civilization**! Historians have noted that the Babylonians thought fish men brought them civilization. The Chinese maintain that their civilization was founded by amphibious beings with the upper bodies of humans and lower bodies of fish. There is also an occurrence of a merman motif found in Assyrian and Phoenician art including coins from Ashdod and Arvad. Clearly, Nimrod — Babylon's civilizer — is Dagon as well. Like the spirit of Nimrod strives to transform ("*civilize*") human beings, he also likes transforming himself! Keep in mind, Satan is the master of deceit; he will wear any **mask**. Likewise, he creates masks of "*Christianity*" ("*civilized morality*") for people, convincing them that the mask is real.

Continuing in his **spiritual masquerade**, Dagon was also known as the Chaldean **fish-man**, Oannes or Oe, who rose out of the depths of the sea to **teach** people every useful **science**. He is now a great **teacher** and a great **civilizer**! In fact, according to the *Encyclopedia of Freemasonry and its Kindred Sciences*, Oannes was the earliest instructor of man in letters, sciences, and arts, especially in architecture, geometry, botany, and agriculture. It is interesting that the title of the mason's encyclopedia indicates that freemasonry, itself, is considered a **science**.

Perhaps the most prominent "*civilizer*" of modern man today is **psychology**, which calls itself **science**, but is really philosophical and religious in nature. Psychology is actually a "*wolf in sheep's clothing,*" and another **mask** for the spirit of Nimrod, transforming the condition of man so they can function in **his civilization**.

Oannes, the **universal teacher**, supposedly had great **knowledge** despite the fact that he was half animal. He was considered the first **Hermes**, (from which we get the word *"hermeneutics,"* meaning the art of **interpreting hidden meaning**) and the first *"founder of the Mysteries"*! Masons are actually honoring Oannes at their grand festival on the day of St. John, *"midsummer-day." "Midsummer"* is set in the Papal calendar as June 24 and is also the day the **sun** is at its greatest altitude. The Babylonians celebrated Tammuz, the false Messiah of the original pagans, on this *"midsummer-day."*

THE FISHERMAN'S RING

Further identification between the Pope and the *"Fish,"* now brings Peter and Christ into the horrifying picture. It may be seen in the ring the Pope proudly wears. Again we see over and over, in order to unite paganism and Christianity into one apostate church, leaders of *"the falling away"* always sought for similarities between the two systems because such allowed the two sides to be merged in a much less obvious way.

H.A. Ironside says that the Pope is *"the direct successor of the high priest of the Babylon Mysteries and the servant of the fish-god Dagon, for whom he wears, like his idolatrous predecessors — **the fisherman's ring**."* The fisherman's ring is also called *"Pescatorio,"* and was the signet ring of official documents signed by the Pope. Private letters of the Pope thus had *"the seal of the fisherman."*

Similarly, in the Roman Empire, gold signet rings were worn as talisman, charms for protection against evil. The raised lettering was reversed so that the ring could be used as a signet.

Since Peter was at one time a fisherman, the people were told that this pagan fish-god ring, with the title *"Pontiff Maximus"* inscribed on it, was associated with Peter's previous occupation. Another similarity the pagans use was that Christ had said He would make Peter a *"fisher of men."* The ring has even born the image of St. Peter casting his nets from a fishing boat.

Such a ring was certainly never worn by Peter the Apostle, and

40 *The Modern Babylon*

no one in the early church ever superstitiously bowed and kissed his ring like faithful Catholics do with the Pope's ring. In fact, he probably didn't even own a ring, for Peter said in Acts 3:6, *"Then Peter said, Silver and gold have I none; but such as I have give I thee: In the name of Jesus Christ of Nazareth rise up and walk."*

Like the pagans linked Peter with Dagon, Jesus Christ Himself (called a **great teacher** and **fisher of men**) has been linked to the fish-god, the false Messiah! New-agers herald the constellation, Pisces, as the sign of the fish and a symbol for the people of God, because humanity supposedly moved into the sign of Pisces about 2,000 years ago, around the time Christ came into the world. Astrologers also say humanity will soon move into the next sign, Aquarius, meaning a time of **peace** and **harmony**. *". . . In Pices the Fishes, he was a fish — Dagon, or Vishnu, the fish-god of the Philistines and Hindoos"* (*"**The Secret Teachings of All Ages**"*, by Manly P. Hall, 33° Freemason, p. XLIX). Ideas connecting Christ with this unholy *"Fish"* are really pointing them toward the Antichrist whom the Bible says will come in the name of **peace**.

THE FALLEN CHURCH

The pallium which the Pope wears over his shoulders as a symbol of his authority is yet further proof of the paganism of the **fallen church**. Unabridged dictionaries define the pallium as a pagan garment worn by the pagan clergy of Greece and Rome before the Christian Era. Hislop says that about the time the Pope took on the title, *"Universal Bishop,"* (*"Universal Overseer"* and *"All-Seeing Janus,"*) the custom of investing the chief bishops with the pallium, which would represent **Papal livery**, began. This also showed that the archbishops share in the plentitude of the Papal office. *"That pallium . . . bound those who received it to act as functionaries of Rome, deriving all their authority from him . . . as the 'Bishop of bishops. . . .'"*

Like the Pope's mitre resembles the mitre of the ancient Dagon, the pallium resembles the ancient Egyptian *"ankh."* The *"ankh"* is the Egyptian symbol meaning *"**life**."* This looped cross that appears as a T supporting a circular shape is the also called the *"tau."* Ancient drawings of Egyptian Gods such as Isis and Horus show them holding the *"ankh"* in virtually every painting found of them. The *"tau"* was also a known symbol of the sun-god, Mithras, and his forerunner, Tummuz. In fertility cults, the *"tau"* represents the union of male and female as a source of creative power. The pallium is thereby, stating that the Pope is the source of life for the church! Jesus said, *". . . I am the **Way**, the **Truth**, and **the Life**: no man cometh unto the Father, but by Me"* (Jn. 14:6).

In addition, the pallium is made of white lamb's wool. Each year on Jan. 21, the day of the Feast of St. Agnes, two baby lambs are *"blessed"* by the Pope in the basilica of St. Agnes of Rome. The two **lambs** are selected as the **choicest** (one could say spotless lambs) among the flock reared in a monastery for this specific purpose. St. Agnes was a celebrated Roman virgin and martyr of the Fourth Century who regularly saw apparitions of Mary, and her name means *"lamb"* or *"victim"* in Latin, and *"pure"* in Greek. When the lambs are brought to St. Agnes Church on their way to the Pope, one is crowned with white roses to signify her virginity (purity) and one with red roses to signify her martyrdom. The Catholic Church should be reminded here that there was only One *"Spotless Lamb."* In addition, the two lambs are placed on the altar where St. Agnes' relics lie, and laid out all night on the supposed tomb of St. Peter — such practices being clear copies of ancient pagan ritual. Hislop called the pallium, *"the visible investiture of these wolves in sheep's clothing."* As well, Tammuz, the false Babylonian Messiah, had long been associated with shepherding and fishing.

The Catholic Church's *"Christian"* explanation connects the lamb's wool with the idea of the Good Shepherd carrying the lost sheep on His shoulders suggesting the Pope's pastoral role as the **icon** of Christ. The problem with this picture is that Jesus said, *"I am the Good Shepherd: the good shepherd giveth his life for the sheep."* (Jn. 10:11) Christ did just that; He gave His Life. No Pope has ever died for his followers, and the Pope was never intended to replace the leading of Jesus Christ in the individual's life. Jesus alone, as Lord and Savior in a person's life, can carry him through. The Catholic Church must wake up! Who was the **One who died** for you? Is He not the **One worthy** of your worship?

THE MYSTERY KEYS

Now, remember those *"mystery keys,"* of the Pope. They show up in even more **imagery of the Papacy**, being as equally famous as the Pope's crown. These are most often seen on the Papal Coat of Arms. The two keys are pictured in saltire form, one crossed over the other to form an X. One key is gold and the other is silver, and a red cord ties them together. Each Pope has his own Coat of Arms, but the **image** of the crossed keys beneath the Pope's crown is the basis for each one. These supposedly represent the *"keys to the Kingdom of Heaven"* spoken of in Matthew 16:19.

This is actually one of the most revealing symbols for the Papacy's role within the Catholic Church because it represents what Catholics claim is Jesus' declaration of **Petrine authority**. It is taken from the rest of Matthew 16:19: *". . . whatever you bind on Earth shall be bound in Heaven, and whatever you loose on Earth shall be loosed in Heaven."* Catholic tradition teaches that the crossed keys symbolized two established jurisdictions — Heaven and Earth. The silver and gold keys are said to represent the two jurisdictions, the silver key symbolizing the power to bind and loose on Earth, and the gold key symbolizing the power to bind and loose in Heaven.

Actually, *"the keys of the Kingdom of Heaven"* do symbolize a type of true Biblical authority, but it is nowhere close to the Catholic interpretation of this verse that is bias to Papal/Petrine authority. In this verse, the *"keys"* represent the authority and power to do the works of Christ, and the word *"keys,"* a symbolism used by Christ, refers back to *"the key of the House of David."*

"And the key of the house of David will I lay upon his shoulder; so he shall open, and none shall shut; and he shall shut, and none

shall open." (Isa. 22:22) In one sense, this was a literal key held by the treasurer of the nations of Israel, but even then, it also referred to authority granted by Christ. Jesus referred to these *"keys"* twice to John the Beloved on the Isle of Patmos, when he said, *". . . and have the keys of hell and of death"* (Rev. 1:18). *"And to the angel of the church in Philadelphia write; These things saith he that is holy, he that is true, he that hath the key of David, he that openeth, and no man shutteth; and shutteth, and no man openeth"* (Rev. 3:7).

The warning to the church is clear: **no man** opens or shuts the Kingdom of Heaven; it must be *"he that hath the key of David."* The first example speaks of *"keys of hell and death"* being held by Christ, but the latter reference of the *"keys"* meant they were shared by **Christ and His Church.** Several things are said here:

KINGDOM OF HEAVEN

1. First, these are the *"keys of the Kingdom of Heaven"* and not the *"key"* to some earthly organization like the Catholic Church or any such Protestant group. The *"Kingdom of Heaven"* is actually the **rule of Christ in the heart and life of the Believer.** It is **spiritual.** Therefore, it is spiritually attained, not gained by **institutional membership** or **religious sacrament.** For instance, being *"baptized into the church"* does not automatically mean you are *"baptized into Christ."* Christ has a *"Heavenly Kingdom."*

2. As well, the *"key"* does not refer to any religious hierarchy. It actually refers to the entirety of the **Body of Christ**, not to just Peter or some successor. The *"key"* belongs to the Body of Christ, of which Peter was only one member. In other words, the power the Catholic Popes and priests claim actually belong to everyone who professes faith in Christ. The Papal government is **stealing** the power and authority of Christ from its members by claiming they are the only ones to whom it belongs.

3. *"The keys to the Kingdom of Heaven"* refers to each and **every Believer**, irrespective of whom they may be, with **Power** and **Authority** given unto each one in order that they may carry out the **Work of God** on Earth and in effect, carry on the work started by Jesus. The True Church of Jesus Christ, whether still bound by the Catholic Church or bound by any Protestant control, needs to take back the *"keys!"* Man should not be allowed to control the Works of God. The *"keys"* have been given unto us, and it is our duty and responsibility to use them.

4. The *"keys"* also specify the **preaching** or **proclamation** of the **Gospel**, whether one-on-one or to a large gathering. Whenever the Believer does this, whether layman or Preacher, he is, in effect, taking the *"key"* and **unlocking the spiritual prison** which binds humanity. When it is accepted, **the Gospel sets the captive free!** What a privilege it is to have the Gospel, as well as the privilege of being used by the Lord to bring others to Salvation. These *"keys"* are not used nearly as much as they ought to be, considering that a great percentage of the world still knows little or nothing about Jesus Christ and **His Power to Save**.

CORRECT DOCTRINE

5. Regrettably, most of the *"keys"* used will not unlock the door, simply because they are the **wrong** *"keys"* — **false doctrine**! You see, **the *"key"* was doctrinal in nature!** The **right** *"Key"* is the **Cross** — both to get in the Kingdom and to start the Work of the Kingdom in your life. In other words, you have to have the right key to get in the car and the right key to start the car. The **Key is the Cross** — both for Salvation and Sanctification!

Again, we see how blasphemous the claim that Janus or the Pope has the *"key"* with *"power to open and shut,"* or *"bind and loose.*" The Lord shows such amazing mercy in so many ways, He knew what terminology would directly refute the lies of the occult and false teachers, so He spoke with clarity through Christ and the Holy Spirit, many times using the exact same terms to expose their error. The pagans claim Peter was the "*rock*", but Jesus said, "**I Am** the **Rock!**"

The pagans claim the Pope is the "*shepherd*", but the Jesus said, "*I Am* the ***Shepherd!***" The pagans claim they possess the creative power of life, but Jesus said, "*I Am* the ***Life!***" The pagans say Janus guards the doors of Heaven, but Jesus said, "*I Am* the ***Door!***" The pagans crown their Priest-Kings, but Jesus is the "***King of kings***," "***Lord of lords***," and the "***High Priest!***" Jesus said, "*I Am that I Am* . . ." (Ex. 3:14). And like Jesus asked his disciples, ". . . *whom do you say that I am?*" (Mat. 16:15), Jesus is asking the world today: "***Whom do you say that I Am?***"

CHAPTER FIVE

Another major attempt made to associate the Pope with the Apostle Peter can be seen in the way the Roman Catholic Church claimed to possess what they call the *"Cathedra of St. Peter"* — *"Peter's chair."* A *"cathedra,"* is the Latin term for the Episcopal chair or throne and is the accepted symbol for the teaching authority of the Roman Catholic Church. When a *"cathedra"* is installed into a church, the church is called a *"cathedral."*

The term *"ex cathedra"* means *"from the throne"* and is used to designate official pronouncements of the Pope as the successor of St. Peter, when he theoretically instructs the whole world in the ways of God. According to Catholic dogma, *"ex cathedra"* statements are *"infallable."*

Remember, when God establishes **Jerusalem** as His city or His church, Satan always sets up **Babylon**, a city *"against the Lord."* Satan has always wanted to take God's place. In his **jealously**, he actually tries to **copy** the very *"throne"* of God that he **coveted** in Heaven.

The Pope's chair of authority refers to his office as the Bishop of Rome as well as the governing head of the Vatican city-state within Rome. The Pope is, thereby, considered a monarch — an **absolute ruler** or king — his home being the Vatican Palace. The Vatican gained its independence from Italy as a sovereign state in 1929. Truly, the Roman Catholic Church desires to establish a religious kingdom and king on earth. But, shouldn't the *"church"* be taking orders from the Throne of Heaven upon which it is the Lord Who sits and speaks Truth? *"And He that sat upon the Throne said, Behold, I make all things new. And he said unto me,* **Write: for these words are true and faithful**" (Rev. 21:5). ***"Ex cathedra"*** is nothing compared to "*It is written.*" You must choose — the Word or the "*chair.*"

PETER?

There was only One who walked perfectly on this Earth — Jesus Christ! No human, even if he was Pope and/or head of the church, has ever lived up to this standard. "*For all have sinned, and come short of the Glory of God*" (Rom. 3:23). And if Christ's words to Peter in Matthew 16:18 made him the first Pope, the problem is even worse than we thought because Peter's very next words denied the heart of the Christian Gospel — they suggested that Christ did not need to go to the Cross! "*Then Peter took Him, and began to rebuke Him, saying, Be it far from Thee, Lord: this shall not be unto Thee*" (Mat. 16:22). The Lord responded immediately with a stinging rebuke to Peter. Christ called Peter, Satan! "*But He turned, and said unto Peter, Get thee behind Me, Satan: thou art an offence unto Me: for thou savourest not the things that be of God, but those that be of men*" (Mat. 16:23). Here we have it — Peter's Satanically-inspired initial statement of "*ex cathedra,*" on faith and morals dealing with the means of salvation and given to the whole church. Clearly, it was not "*infallible*" but total heresy.

In just the next chapter, Peter seriously errs again with another misguided edict, which put Christ on the same level with Moses and Elias: "*Then answered Peter, and said unto Jesus, Lord, it is good for us to be here: if thou wilt, let us make here three Tabernacles; one for Thee, and one for Moses, and one for Elias*" (Mat. 17:4). This time it was God from Heaven who rebuked the "*new pope.*" "*While He yet spake, behold, a bright cloud overshadowed them: and behold a Voice out of the cloud, which said, This is My Beloved Son, in Whom I am well pleased; hear ye Him*" (Mat. 17:5).

And yet, the next thing we know we find Peter, in fear for his life, denying with "*oaths and curses*" that he knew Christ at all — again, a statement on faith and morals to the entire church in denial of Christ Himself (Mk. 14:66-72). As well, as we have already stated, Paul had to rebuke Peter very strongly at another time he was in error. *"But when Peter was come to Antioch, I withstood him to the face, because he was to be blamed"* (Gal. 2:11). So if we want to say that the popes are the successors of Peter, they certainly do not possess *"infallibility"* since Peter could not have passed on what he, himself, did not possess.

THE CHAIR

Until the year 1662, the Catholic Church actually thought that there was proof, not only of St. Peter erecting the actual material *"chair"* in the Vatican, but of his sitting in it as well. Until that year, the very chair on which they believed and had others believe Peter had sat was regularly shown and exposed for public adoration on the day of *"The Festival of St. Peter's Chair."* This festival is annually celebrated in Rome on January 18 as an act of gratitude for the founding of the papacy and the "***mother church***." It takes place in St. Peter's Basilica as one of the few functions held in that hallowed cathedral.

Amusingly, however, while the chair was being cleaned one day, *"the twelve labors of Hercules unluckily appeared on it"* — *"unlucky,"* that is, for those preserving the lie that Peter was the first Pope. Hercules was the Roman name for the greatest **hero** of Greek **mythology** — Heracles. His *"twelve labors,"* which have been associated with the twelve signs of the zodiac, made Hercules the perfect example of the Greek principle called *"pathos"* — the experience of virtuous struggle leading to fame and, in Hercules' case, **immortality**. In fact, *"pathos,"* meaning *"sufferings"* in Greek, was unapologetically considered an **appeal to the pride of life**, and it was one of Aristotle's (a great philosopher of the world and prime adviser to Alexander the Great) teachings on *"rhetoric,"* the art of **persuasion**. Obviously, the moral of Hercules' story does not fit the Doctrine of the Cross of Christ; such **heretical parables** would not have been tolerated by Peter or any of the other disciples.

CATHOLIC ENCYCLOPEDIA

The Catholic Encyclopedia also shows a photograph of Peter's supposed *"chair,"* mentioning that the plates on its front display commonly recognized **animal-like** characters of mythology and the fabled *"Labors of Hercules."* Keeping in mind the pagan carvings connected with Hercules, it is interesting to notice a statement made in another volume of the Catholic Encyclopedia: *"Gilgamesh, whom mythology transformed into a Babylonian Hercules — would then be the person designated by the Biblical Nemrod (Nimrod)."*

Gilgamesh was the **semidivine king** of Erech, a city of southern Babylonia. This would mean that the *"chair"* glorifying this Gilgamesh was also signifying Nimrod, the sun-god (a.k.a. Baal), and according to the Greek idea of *"pathos,"* portrayed him as a man who worked his way to **godhood**. Was the man of this *"chair"* destined to become a god?

Even more, if you look at plural meanings of the word *"Baal,"* many include the **feminine** gender. The various titles of the *"Baal-gods"* or *"Baal-goddesses"* were considered the **Lord or Lady** of a particular place. Maybe *"**Our Lady**"* — the Roman Catholic deified version of Mary — will eventually take the *"chair."* Considering these chilling implications, there is certainly no reason to believe that the so-called *"Chair of St. Peter"* originated in Christianity.

And yet, there is still another embarrassment to those who profess *"Peter's chair."* A latter claimed *"chair"* seemed to have come from Muslims. In Arabic, this well-known sentence of the Koran, *"There is no God but God, and Mahomet is His Prophet,"* was found on the back of it. A scientific commission appointed by Pope Paul in July of 1968 has officially reported that no part of the chair is old enough to date from the days of Peter; carbon dating (radio-active carbon in wood measured to determine how long ago a tree was cut) and other tests indicated that the chair is no older than the Ninth Century.

THE CHAIR OF PETER?

Another term used for the Vatican, the *"Chair of Peter,"* and/or the throne of the Pope, is the Latin phrase, *"Sancta Sedes,"* meaning "*Holy Seat*" or "*Holy See*," from which the Pope's purportedly "*infallable*" teachings come. In the Old Testament, Jerusalem (a.k.a. Zion or the City of David) was actually called a "***holy city***" because it represented God and His people. An inscription on Jewish coins was "*Jerusalem the Holy*." Arabs still call it "*el Kuds*", "*the Holy*."

Today, the Lord's "*Jerusalem*" has more of a spiritual meaning and refers to the true Church of the Lord Jesus Christ, the true Kingdom of God that is made "*holy*" by the Blood of the Lamb. "*And I John saw* **the Holy City, new Jerusalem**, *coming down from God out of Heaven, prepared as a bride adorned for her husband*" (Rev. 21:2). Satan, in his **greed**, desires to rule his own "*holy city*," "*against the Lord*" — a profile of which the "*Holy See*" fits perfectly.

Adding to this framework, Old Testament Zion was actually a hill on the north part of Jerusalem. The temple of Jerusalem, built upon the hill of Moriah, was either a part of "*Mount Zion*" or adjoining to it. Ironically, the Vatican was originally called "*Vaticanus Mons*," meaning "*Vatican hill*," in Latin. In fact, both Rome and Jerusalem have been called "*the city of seven hills*," as they both sit on seven mountains. Either way (since today Israel and the physical city of Jerusalem rejects Christ), it is notable that the Bible reveals that "***the woman***" — the false religion of Babylon — will sit on a **city of seven hills**: "*Here is the mind which hath wisdom. The seven heads are seven mountains on which the woman sitteth*" (Rev. 17:9). The earthly "*holy city on a hill*" is not truly holy. On the other hand, the true "*holy city*" is the "*heavenly Jerusalem*," and its **counterfeit clone**, Satan's Modern Babylon, is marked for the wrath of God. "*And there followed another Angel, saying,* **Babylon is fallen**, *is fallen,* **that great city . . .** " (Rev. 14:8).

KINGDOM NOW?

Church, this is why it is so important that we are not looking to establish the Kingdom of God on Earth — any "***kingdom now***" thinking is dangerous! Remember, this is why Israel didn't recognize Jesus the first time He came. The Jews wanted Him to set up an *"earthly kingdom!"* Jesus, however, came to establish a *"heavenly kingdom."*

The Bible clearly teaches that Satan, as the *"god of this world"* (an authority allowed by the Lord in this time period), is the one trying to establish a kingdom on Earth over which he will declare himself god, and according to Scripture, this will happen. If you believe Scripture, you have to believe this. The Lord will not set up His Kingdom on Earth (the New Heaven and New Earth) until the Millennial Reign of Christ which the Bible teaches will not occur until after the Antichrist has ruled from his earthy throne. The world will see the kingdom of the Antichrist on Earth before it will see the Kingdom of Christ on Earth. The Antichrist will make his debut first. Therefore, any so-called *"kingdom of god"* presently established on Earth can only be the kingdom of the Antichrist. All the happenings of the world — politically, socially, religiously, economically, educationally, etc. — can only conform to this effort. If we aid this effort, we are aiding and abetting the enemy.

The Bible has repeatedly warned us not to develop a love relationship with this present world; all of its actions and triumphs will ultimately work in accordance with Satan himself. *"Love not the world, neither the things that are in the world. If any man love the world, the love of the Father is not in him"* (I Jn. 2:15).

The efforts of true Christians must be towards building Christ's *"Heavenly Kingdom,"* (the New Jerusalem) thereby, spiritually **removing people** from the **world system**. Meanwhile, under a guise of **heroically noble** and **charitable deeds**, plenty of ecumenical *"ONE"* movements and *"P.E.A.C.E."* campaigns are well on their way toward establishing world unity. The question is: *"**Who hasn't gone global?**"* Amazingly, what are now being considered by some to be the church's greatest enemies are called *"**global giants**."* The modern *"church,"* both Catholic and Protestant alike, is defending *"global"* rather than *"Bible!"* Unfortunately, it sounds as though the light has already become dark!

IDOLS!

Another clear indicator of Babylonian paganism in the Roman Catholic Church can be seen in some of its blatant physical expressions of worship and the objects of this worship — specifically, the **bowing, kneeling,** and **kissing** of **idols**! What does the Bible say about such worship? *"Their land also is full of **idols**; they **worship the work of their own hands**, that which their own fingers have made"* (Isa. 2:8).

An idol really constitutes anything made by man — whether material or conceptual — that acquires worship belonging to the Lord alone. You see, idols are technically in a person's heart, but they may take on **visible representations** as they did among the ancient pagans. Astonishingly, Roman Catholics have likewise made quite an open display of their idolatrous hearts. However, one need not think it strange considering the other heathen practices which were absorbed into Catholicism.

Such idolatry was part of Baal worship — the very worship repeatedly condemned in the Bible. In the days of Elijah, multitudes had bowed to and kissed Baal or one of his numerous **symbols** — the identical rite of which we are speaking. God said *"Yet I have left me seven thousand in Israel, all the knees which have not **bowed unto Baal**, and every mouth which hath not **kissed him**"* (I Ki. 19:18). In the Semitic language, *"Baal"* meant *"possessor,"* *"lord,"* or *"owner."*

According to place and circumstances, Baal-worship has been described in many ways; some cases include: sun-worship, moon-worship, Cid-worship, Melek (Moloch)-worship (symbolized as a snake, bear, lion, or owl) and Hadad (Adad) -worship (symbolized as a dragon, lion, bull, or lightning bolt). The Baal of Lebanon was probably Cid, *"the hunter,"* the partly fish-shaped Baal of Arvad, Dagon, and the Baal of Harran, the moon-god named Sin. In Sabean Minaean cities and in Chanaanite, Phoenician, and Palmyrene shrines, Baal was the sun-god. The chief Baal among the Syrians seems to have been Hadad, the *"shaper of elemental forces."*

The Semites, most likely moved by their desire to secure the protection of the local Baal for their children, always showed a preference for names compounded with Baal: Hasdrubal (*'Azrû Bá'ál*), Hannibal (*Hanni Bá'ál*), Baltasar, or Belshazzar (Bel-sar-Ushshur). There are many examples like these from many cultures; they are recorded in ancient writings, ancient inscriptions, and the Bible. Remember, too, that Baal was female or had a female counterpart in many societies.

Essentially, Baal worship was thereby nothing more or less than the worship of the sun-god (ancient Nimrod in deified form), just as it was an ancient custom to kiss **statues, images, or emblems** of him as well. "*. . . I have reserved to myself seven thousand men, who have not bowed the knee to the **image of Baal**"* (Rom. 11:4).

Apparently, a **desensitization to image-worship** began from the earliest Babylon and perfectly plays into the plans of the Antichrist who will "*. . . cause that as many as would not **worship** the **image of the beast** should be killed*" (Rev. 13:15) and "*. . . **receive** his **mark** in his **forehead**, or in his **hand**"* (Rev. 14:9). A "*mark*," as well, is a symbolic image or **emblem** of **loyalty** to an object.

In one of Nimrod's mystery forms (as Tammuz), he was represented as a **calf**. In the Old Testament, when God's people went after other gods, statues of calves were made, worshipped, and kissed! "*When Ephraim spake trembling, he exalted himself in Israel; but when he offended in Baal, he died. And now they sin more and more, and have made them **molten images** of their **silver**, and idols according to their **own understanding**, all of it the **work of the craftsmen**: they say of them, Let the men that **sacrifice kiss the calves**"* (Hos. 13:1-2).

It is hard to imagine that anyone would choose to represent any all-powerful god as a man or especially as an animal, but in writing to the Church of Rome, Paul warned that some would: "*And changed the glory of the **uncorruptible** God into an image made like to **corruptible man**, and to **birds**, and **fourfooted beasts**, and **creeping things**"* (Rom. 1:23).

Old Testament prophets, as well, spoke against such idolatry: *"Lest ye corrupt yourselves, and make you a graven image, the **similitude of any figure**, the **likeness** of **male** or **female**, The **likeness** of any **beast** that is on the Earth, the **likeness** of any **winged fowl** that flieth in the air, The likeness of **any thing** that creepeth on the ground, the **likeness** of any **fish** that is in the waters beneath the Earth: And lest thou lift up thine eyes unto Heaven, and when thou **seest** the **sun**, and the **moon**, and the **stars**, even all the host of heaven, shouldest be **driven to worship** them, and **serve them** . . ."* (Deut. 4:16-19). *"To **whom then will ye liken God**? or **what likeness will ye compare unto Him**? The workman melteth a graven image, and the goldsmith spreadeth it over with **gold**, and casteth **silver chains**"* (Isa. 40:18-19).

NIMROD

One direct link to the pagan Nimrod was the finding of the statue of Jupiter in Rome many centuries ago. The large bronze statue in all its native ugliness was slightly **altered** and **renamed** "*St. Peter*." Jupiter was the Roman name and form of Tammuz, so it is obvious that the very **statue** still standing today and **posing** as St. Peter is utilized for the same old worship of Nimrod, the same old worship of Baal! In fact, many pagan idols have been given **new identities** as **saints**, but this religious *"witness protection program"* has clearly failed. It is unfortunate that many Catholics have not yet recognized these true identities. The statue of *"St. Peter"* is still looked upon with the most profound veneration. The foot of this statue has been kissed so many times by devoted followers that the toes are nearly worn away. (*Ancient Monuments of Rome* p.79)

Actually, any "*saint*" is one among the many idols of the Catholic Church. In Catholicism, only a person of "***extraordinary holiness***" can become a saint. Someone being considered for sainthood will have his/her life examined including writings, teachings, **heroic** acts, and outstanding **virtues** to see if he is **worthy** of such a title. Apparently, evidence which indicates that the *"chair of Peter"* told the story of Hercules is not so far-fetched. The candidate must also

perform a miracle after his death as a result of his **intercession** with God. Upon tangible manifestation of the miracle, the candidate is called "*blessed*" (as in the Blessed Mother Teresa) and continues on in his or her quest toward sainthood. How blasphemous is this claim since it is **Christ** who is our **Intercessor** at God's Throne, not **dead men**!

On certain occasions the statue of St. Peter is also dressed with rich papal robes and three-tiered papal crowns. It is little wonder, then, that faithful followers also **kiss** and **bow to the Pope**. You see, the **Pope himself**, is just **one more image, one more idol of worship**! The Pope, in reality, is the representative, not of Christ or Peter the apostle, but the god of "*Mystery Babylon*"! So, to those who understand the "*mystery*," it is not a mystery at all! The particularly scary thing about this idol, however, is that **the Pope is the idol which best prepares the world to worship the Antichrist!** In fact, as we saw with the recent death of Pope John Paul II, the **world is now comfortable paying homage to a man — the Pope!**

BOW THE KNEE

It is interesting that the Bible uses some specific terminology regarding the act of bowing. Over and over again, the Bible uses the phrase, "***bowing the knee***" which actually indicates the act of kneeling! For instance, "*And Pharaoh took off his ring from his hand, and put it upon Joseph's hand . . . and they cried before him, **Bow the knee**: and he made him ruler over all the land of Egypt*" (Gen. 41:42-43). As well, we have already seen it used in regard to Baal worship: "*. . . **bowed the knee** to the image of Baal*" (Rom. 11:4).

The term is even used to demonstrate worship of the True Christ: "*For it is written, As I live, saith the Lord, every **knee** shall **bow** to me, and every **tongue** shall **confess** to God*" (Rom. 14:11). In general, kneeling is viewed as a sign of extreme respect and honor; kissing would certainly mean no less. Notice here, too, that every tongue will confess Jesus as Lord. Those whose mouths are used to kissing Baal would be better off practicing the proper confession of the Lord lest they stumble on the words in last days.

Catholics also stand and kneel throughout their service or mass as it shows the ultimate **posture** of **submission** and **surrender** — supposedly, in the words of one Catholic, as "*. . . a total submission of our minds and hearts to the true Presence of Christ.*" The problem, though, is that the "*true Presence of Christ,*" according to Catholic tradition, is yet another idol — a **piece** of **bread** which has allegedly become the literal Christ.

We have also seen kneeling in the "*dubbing*" of medieval **knights** as they are made ready for **militant service**.

The world just witnessed three American presidents (George Bush Sr., George Bush Jr., and Bill Clinton) "*bow the knee*" in prayer before the body of Pope John Paul II. In fact, we saw many world leaders bow at the funeral of the Pope. How many in the modern "*church*" would have "*bowed the knee*" had they attended the funeral? How many would have addressed the Pope as "*Your Holiness*" as we have seen among many world leaders (including former president Ronald Reagan) throughout history? Just recently, President George Bush presented Pope John Paul II with the Presidential Medal of Freedom which included a citation on the medal calling John Paul II "*His Holiness.*" Ignorance is not an excuse for idolatry.

CHAPTER SIX

IDOLS

Continuing in the horror of such shameless idolatry, the Roman Catholic Church has also adopted the pagan custom of holding **grand religious processions** in which idols are **carried** and **displayed** in all their **ceremonial vanity**. Such Disney-like **parades**, complete with **music, dancing**, and other **entertainments**, are purely pagan in origin, yet are a regular part of Catholic ceremonies. In the Fifteenth Century B.C., an image of the Babylonian goddess Ishtar (Semiramis) was carried with great pomp and splendor from Babylon to Egypt. Such was also seen in Greece, Egypt, Ethiopia, Mexico, and many other pagan countries in olden times. A comparison of the ancient Egyptian processions from over three thousand years ago and the Papal processions of today prove to be exact copies of one another.

The Bible clearly shows the folly of those who think any good can come from idols — idols so powerless and fragile they must be carried! *"And the rest of the men which were not killed by these plagues yet repented not of the works of their hands, that they should not worship devils, and idols of **gold**, and **silver**, and **brass**, and **stone**, and of **wood**: which **neither can see, nor hear, nor walk**"* (Rev. 9:20).

Isaiah, in direct reference to the gods of Babylon, had this to say: *"They lavish gold out of the bag, and weigh silver in the balance, and hire a goldsmith; and he maketh it a god: they fall down, yea, they worship. They **bear him upon the shoulder**, they **carry him** and set him in his place, and he standeth; from his place shall he not remove: yea, one shall cry unto him, yet **can he not answer,*** *nor save him out of his trouble*" (Isa. 46:6-7).

Furthermore, the Bible teaches that those who worship idols will become like those idols (Ps. 115:8; Jer. 2:5). In other words, those who worship these deaf, mute, and lame idols will become spiritual impotents as well. The warning is: "*. . . if the blind shall lead the blind, both shall fall into the ditch*" (Mat. 15:14).

THE PARADE

Yet, even so-called secular environments "*love a parade.*" Social psychologists say that parades can **create** a sense of **community** where even among cities of thousands, a "*small-town*" atmosphere can be produced. Other experts say a parade is really a primitive mating ritual in which looking at an object is the first act of **loving** it and building the desire to **follow** it and "*join in the dance.*"

You see, Satan desires to put an idol in front of a man's eye so that he will **covet**, **imitate**, and **follow** it. A visible image acts as sort of an outlet for worship as regards idols of the heart. "*. . . Thus saith the Lord GOD; Every man of the house of Israel that setteth up his **idols** in his **heart**, and putteth the **stumblingblock of his iniquity before his face**, and cometh to the Prophet; I the LORD will answer him that cometh according to the multitude of his idols*" (Ezek. 14:4).

In fact, some form of such processions, which proudly **flaunt idols**, can be seen across practically all times and cultures — whether along the Nile in Egypt or the "*red carpet*" in America.

And none the less, the so-called "*church*" of Rome insists upon its spectacle even to the point of **carrying the Pope!** As heathen men bore the idol-god "*upon the shoulders,*" men also carry the idol-Pope "*upon the shoulders.*" The heathen people would "*fall down*" and worship their idols like people bow before Popes as they are carried by on occasion today. And to top it all off, the Pope is cloaked with **riches**, just as the heathens of olden times lavished **gold** and **silver** on their idol-god.

The sad thing is the true blessing that Catholic people will miss in this futile work. It is the Lord Jesus Christ alone upon whom one should lavish with the riches of pure worship. *". . . there came a woman having an alabaster box of ointment of spikenard very precious; and she brake the box, and poured it on His head"* (Mk. 14:3).

TWISTED SCRIPTURE!

And while one would hope that such idolatry could be considered unintentional or accidental, the truth is that many versions of the **Roman Catholic Bible** (*The New American Bible* being the most commonly used Roman Catholic text), based on the **Catechism**, have purposely changed the Ten Commandments in order to allow the practice of this dreadful sin. The Second Commandment forbidding the making of idols is completely removed, and the last Commandment is split into two separate commandments. This way it still appears to have the full Ten Commandments like the real Bible.

There could be nothing more evil than the deliberate **twisting of Scripture** (whether in actual word or interpretation of the word); it is the strike of that deceitful serpent, the devil, as the injection of spiritual poison working spiritual death in its victim: *"Now the serpent was more cunning than any . . . And he said unto the woman, 'Yea, **hath God said** . . . ?'"* (Gen. 3:1).

Therefore, God has left a clear message to those who attempt to **modify His Word**: *"For I testify unto every man that heareth the words of the Prophecy of this Book, If any man shall add unto these things, **God shall add unto him the plagues that are written in this Book**"* (Rev. 22:18).

62 The Modern Babylon

The Bible's Ten Commandments (Ex. 20:1-17):	Roman Catholic Bible's Ten Commandments (based on the Catechism):
1. I am the Lord thy God, thou shalt have no other gods before me.	1. I am the Lord your God. You shall not have strange Gods before me.
2. **Thou shall not make unto thee any graven image.**	2. You shall not take the name of the Lord your God in vain.
3. Thou shall not take the name of the Lord thy God in vain.	3. Remember to keep holy the Lord's Day.
4. Remember the Sabbath Day to keep it holy.	4. Honor your father and your mother.
5. Honor thy father and thy mother.	5. You shall not kill.
6. Thou shall not kill.	6. You shall not commit adultery.
7. Thou shall not commit adultery.	7. You shall not steal.
8. Thou shall not steal.	8. You shall not bear false witness against your neighbor.
9. Thou shall not bear false witness.	9. You shall **not covet** your neighbor's wife.
10. Thou shall not covet.	10. You shall **not covet** your neighbor's goods.

PAGANS

Why? One is forced to ask this question regarding the complete omission of the Second Commandment in the Roman Catholic Bible. The ever-increasingly clear answer is because Roman Catholicism has adopted the use of graven-image idolatry in their worship. The venerated **statues** of Roman Catholicism plainly display the violation of this law of God just *"as the pagans of old* *had idols and statues of their gods or goddesses."* In many cases, the very same statue that was once worshipped as a **pagan god** is now worshipped under the name of a Christian "***saint***," a prime example being the statue of Jupiter renamed as St. Peter.

This "*Christianized*" devotion to Satan's old pagan gods continues in disguise as, through the centuries, more and more statues have been made and venerated in Catholicism. Churches in Europe contain as many as two, three, and four thousand statues.

The Babylonians believed that their gods and goddesses had once been **living heroes on earth** (extraordinary men) that had since been transferred to a higher plane and become sort of a **demi-god class**, very similar to what the Catholics believe about their "*saints*." It is a well-known fact, too, that even secular Greeks and Romans were obsessed with the human form; they considered the perfection they perceived to be nothing less than divine.

So human beings, who have always preferred the worship of "*self*," have gone right ahead and made their idol-statues to look like men too. The very nature of a statue, in effect, implies that one knows something of how the object of worship appears. Apparently, the pagans as well as the Catholics think that gods look like men. And interestingly, Roman statues were often the combined representation of a god and a great leader such as an emperor or pope.

BABYLONIAN WORSHIP

The Vatican itself is packed full of strikingly impressive statues occupying every nook and corner. Every few feet you walk, you make eye contact with another depicted "*saint*," making it truly easy to believe that these heroes of the past are indeed watching over you. One might experience the same feeling upon viewing the founding fathers of Mt. Rushmore. Simply the massive size of many of the Vatican statues (not to mention their beauty) can surely take your breath away, just as many of the cathedrals, paintings, and other works of art in the Vatican. Many are covered in **brilliant gold** as well. In fact, much of the Vatican is drenched in gold, perfectly aligning with the pagan belief that gold was the "*flesh*" of the sun-god. Such awe-inspiring structures truly seem "*larger than life*," so it is no wonder that the artists of the day were considered **geniuses**; their **creative works** could literally stir worship in the heart of men.

Even without the statues, Roman Catholics **honor** and **pray** to various "*saints*." Now these "*saints*," according to Catholic teaching, are martyrs or other notable people of the "*church*" who have died and whom a Pope has declared worthy of sainthood. But again, the idea of **petitioning** saints was nothing more than an adopted pagan custom, taking us back to Babylon, the "*mother*" of false religion.

We find that people honored and prayed to a **plurality of gods** from even the earliest times, and the Babylonian system, in fact, developed until it had some 5,000 gods and goddesses, each associated with a particular season, event, occupation, emotion, or other human happening. Every month and every day of the month was under the protection of a specific deity, and like the worship of the Babylonian Trinity, these gods spread to every nation. For instance, the Buddhists in China worship various deities such as the god of war, the goddess of sailors, even the gods of special neighborhoods. And yes, the pagans continued to worship their chief "*Peter-gods*" ("*father-gods*" and/or "*interpreter-gods*"), but they also worshipped these lesser gods, considering them a quick link for **aid** in particular "*felt needs*." It appears, as well, that in the Babylonian system these **divine mediators** did not undermine the authority of any chief god. In other words, they could be worshipped in addition to, rather than instead of, the chief gods.

GODS AND GODDESSES

"*Janus*" was the god of doors and gates. "*Brighit*" was the goddess of smithcraft and poetry. "*Minerva*" was the goddess of schools, wisdom, handicrafts, and musicians. "*Venus*" was the goddess of sexual love and birth. "*Juno Regina*" was the goddess of womanhood, marriage, and maternity. "*Cronus*" was the guardian of oaths. "*Apollo*" was the god of medicine and health. "*Cestor*" and "*Pollux*" were the protectors of Rome and of travelers at sea. "*Vesla*" was the goddess of bakers and sacred fires. "*Bellona*" was the goddess of war. "*Hercules*" was the god of joy and wine. "*Mercury*" was the patron deity of merchants, orators, and thieves. The list goes on and on. Basically anything imagined had a "*ministering*" agent to assure its livelihood.

When Rome conquered the world, this system involving the **governing gods of everyday life** was absorbed into Rome's Catholic "*church*." Catholics are, in fact, taught to pray to certain "*saints*" for help with certain afflictions, and Catholic calendars designate certain days for certain "*saints.*" And just as the pagans believed in divinities associated with various occupations, days, ideals, talents, etc., so did Catholicism, thus the tradition of calling them "***patron saints***" — "Patron" meaning "*father*" in Latin.

These "*patron saints*" were thereby, the **guardians** and **protectors** (the fathers) over specified areas of life. The Roman Catholic Church has designated a hundred or more "*saints*" to whom the people are to pray — forty or more for specified **helps**. And sadly, even though most Protestants understand the obvious idol worship of such "***saintly***" **gods**, the Protestant Church often fails to recognize that they follow exactly the same spirit when they primarily confer with their own **idols of a** "*good*" **name** — education, intellect, charisma, science, art, and strategic thinking — to name a few. In fact, many mistakenly believe that good-standing with these demigods will secure their standing with the one true Father, just like the Catholics believe about their "*saints*."

SAINTS?

This method of substituting "*saints*" in the place of the pagan idol-gods became so popular that by the Tenth Century, 25,000 "*saints*" had been canonized by the Roman Catholic Church. Since the new pagan converts had been naturally reluctant to part with their old *"gods,"* it was the easiest way to increase the numbers in the church and bring the masses under the **universal roof of Catholicism** (the word *"catholic"* meaning *"universal"* or indicating *"universal acceptance"*). And are not most somewhat resistant to the idea of giving up former securities and/or creature comforts to follow Christ; isn't this part of true Christianity?

But as we can see, for the sake of numbers and power, we have had false shepherds throughout church history play this same old trick of allowing new converts to believe that Christianity does not include forsaking the **gods of this world**. Certainly, such can be seen throughout denominations of the church world today as pastors preach the *"greed gospel"* of false prosperity and focus their congregations on *"living their best life now."* It is easy to see why this type of thinking would be pagan rather than Christian, for how is one who is concerned with *"living their best life now"* possibly able to count the cost and *"take up their cross?"*

But the greedy leadership in the Church of Rome was greatly pleased with its mixture of pagan and *"Christian"* creeds that helped to **swell its numbers**, and as *"the great falling away"* fell further and further, the lesser idol-gods of practical human affairs were allowed to ascend to higher positions in the **Roman system**. We can now plainly see that whenever *"experiential"* Christianity replaces *"doctrinal"* Christianity, it has followed the example of Rome and her modern Church of Babylon which has no problem allowing an **all-inclusive** and **falsely-unified religion** to flourish as long as she ultimately controls it.

DOCTRINAL COMPROMISE

Doctrinal compromise, no matter how worthy the cause seems, will always bring a severe **lack of spiritual discernment** in the body because accurate discernment ultimately comes from accurate Doctrine. And unfortunately, as history has repeatedly shown and will show again, compromising the truth of God's Word always brings bondage, not liberation. Certainly it is a mandate of Christ to help those in need, but the Church should never allow the ministering of the physical need to distract from ministering the spiritual need — the clear Doctrine of the Gospel (Christ and Him Crucified).

The **original compromisers** of Rome, however, did everything possible to help the blending process, so long as it increased church attendance. One way they did such was by substituting the *"Christian"* name (or saint's name) that sounded as close as possible to the name of the specific pagan god it would replace. For example, the goddess Victoria of the Basses-Alpis was renamed as St. Victoria, Osiris as St. Onuphris, Cheron as St. Ceraunos, Artemis as St. Artemidos, Dionysus as St. Dionysus, Apollo as St. Apolinaris, Mars as St. Martine, and Brighit as St. Bridget.

In pagan days Brighit (the daughter of the sun god, represented with a child in her arms), was served by **vestal virgins** who tended the sacred fires of divine inspiration at her chief temple at Kildare. When the Church's days of *"falling away"* came, the **pagan temple became a convent**, and her vestals became **nuns** who continued to tend the ritual fire dedicated to the goddess, only the fire was now renamed, *"St. Bridget's Fire."* (This also reveals the true origin of the Catholic convent since there is not the slightest hint of foundations for such an organization in the Bible.)

The best preserved ancient temple remaining in Rome — the Pantheon — was originally dedicated to *"Jove and all the gods"* according to the inscription over its *"portico"* (covered entrance). It was later reconstructed by Pope Boniface IV and dedicated to *"the Mother of God and all the Saints."* Another pagan temple at Rome, one sacred to the *"Bona Dea"* (*"the good goddess"*), was *"Christianized"* and dedicated to the Virgin Mary. The church of St. Apollinaris now stands in a place formerly sacred to the god Apollo, and where the ancient temple of Mars stood, now stands the Church of St. Martine.

The leaders hoped that their clever name game would dispel the evidence, but Catholicism has been found guilty, far beyond all reasonable doubt, of a practice repeatedly condemned in the Bible — the worship of "***other gods***." "*Take heed to yourselves, that your **heart be not deceived**, and ye turn aside, and **serve other gods**, and worship them*" (Deut. 11:16). We serve idol-gods from our hearts, so we must continually check our hearts to make sure they have not caused us to serve any other than Jesus Christ.

THE WORD OF GOD

According to the Bible, **all true Christians are Saints** — I want to say that again — according to the Bible, all true Christians are Saints. Why — because their Righteousness is determined by the Blood of the Lamb, not a Pope or any other religious person. And furthermore, there is not one verse of Scripture in the Bible even remotely indicating that a person becomes a saint after he is dead! In fact, the Bible teaches that your Salvation and Standing with God are determined before you die; **nothing can be fixed or changed after death**. You will either wake up in Heaven or in Hell; there is no in-between, and there is no communication with those still alive on this Earth.

In the Scriptures, all references to Saints pertain to living people — never, never, the dead. "*Paul, an Apostle of Jesus Christ by the Will of God, to the Saints which are at Ephesus, and to the faithful in Christ Jesus*" (Eph. 1:1). "*Paul and Timotheus, the servants of Jesus Christ, to all the Saints in Christ Jesus which are at Philippi, with the Bishops and Deacons*" (Phil. 1:1).

The Early Christians in the Church at Rome were called saints: "*To all that be in Rome, Beloved of God, called to be Saints: Grace to you and peace from God our Father, and the Lord Jesus Christ*" (Rom. 1:7). "*Salute Philologus, and Julia, Nereus, and his sister, and Olympas, and all the Saints which are with them*" (Rom. 16:15).

The Christians who lived in Corinth were called Saints as well: "*Unto the church of God which is at Corinth, to them that are Sanctified in Christ Jesus, called to be Saints, with all that in every place call upon the Name of Jesus Christ our Lord, both theirs and ours"* (I Cor. 1:2). *"Paul, an Apostle of Jesus Christ by the Will of God, and Timothy our brother, unto the Church of God which is at Corinth, with all the Saints which are in all Achaia"* (II Cor. 1:1).

Therefore, if you want a true "*saint*" to pray for you, you should find a Christian to join you in prayer. This is a true form of Biblical intercessory prayer.

COMMUNICATION WITH THE DEAD?

However, when we try to contact people who have died, we are "***communing with the dead***," a practice repeatedly forbidden in God's Word because it is a form of spiritism and divination. *"And when they shall say unto you, Seek unto them that have **familiar spirits**, and unto wizards that peep, and that mutter: should not a people seek unto their God? **for the living to the dead**? To the Law and to the Testimony: if they speak not according to this Word, it is because there is **no light in them**"* (Isa. 8:19-20).

Any contact with dead people is demonic no matter how "*holy*" the posing demon seems. Yet, Catholics habitually recite the Apostle's Creed which says, *"We believe . . . in the communion of saints . . . ,"* having reference, not only to the living, but to the "*departed*" as well. It is considered "*. . . a mutual sharing in help, satisfaction, prayer, and other good works, a **mutual communication**" (New Catholic Encyclopedia*, Vol. 4 Page. 41). *"The underlying **doctrine of the patrons** is that of the communion of the saints, or the **bond of spiritual union** existing **between God's servants on earth, in heaven, or in purgatory**. The saints are thereby regarded as the **advocates** and **intercessors** of those who are making their **earthly pilgrimage**" (The Catholic Encyclopedia*, Volume XI-Online Edition).

Clearly, Catholics believe these "*patrons*," these "*god-fathers*," (living "*godfathers*" play a part in Catholic tradition as well) can speak to the Lord on their behalf, but the Father provided only **One Advocate** with Him, and that One, Jesus Christ, is all we need: *"My little children, these things write I unto you, that ye sin not. And if* *any man sin, we have* **an Advocate** *with the Father,* **Jesus Christ the Righteous**" (I Jn. 2:1).

CHAPTER SEVEN

SALVATION?

The Catholic emphasis on the *"Saints"* seems somewhat unwarranted until this particular tradition is viewed in the light of the actual Catholic definition of salvation. You see, Catholics have always believed that salvation is a **process** as opposed to the Bible's teaching of an instantaneous transference from death to life. It is a practice of choosing good over evil and bringing life (salvation) through death (self-sacrifice). In other words, salvation comes through one's **good works**.

This is why the *"Saints"* became quite important guides along the believer's **journey** of conversion. Each *"Saint"* has a particular **area of expertise** that can **provide aid** to the Catholic in accomplishing his/her selected good works! It is interesting that the modern church many times seeks *"experts"* and *"professionals"* to help them accomplish the *"works of God"* as well. The Catholic's *"works of goodness"* are like stepping stones along the Catholic **transforming path of salvation** — whether performing a sacrament, feeding the hungry, praying, or choosing to forgive another person — and each of such *"saving"* events, according to Catholic teaching, brings an individual to an **experiential** contact with God at the same time.

Good works can certainly give someone a warm-fuzzy feeling inside, but does that feeling necessarily indicate the Presence of God, especially when Jesus said that even wicked men are capable of giving good gifts? *"If ye then, being evil, know how to give **good gifts** unto your children . . ."* (Mat. 7:11).

Regardless, the Catholic Church teaches one to equate good humanitarian feelings with the Spirit of God. And such experiential contact also serves to reassure the Catholic believer that their salvation is, in fact, being accomplished. It is easier to believe in something you can feel.

The Bible, on the other hand, never even hints that our works can cause us to have a *"saving"* experience with God, and while Biblical Salvation and a continued Christian Life certainly brings personal experience with Jesus, the Christian's experience of Salvation is complete upon one's expressed Faith in Christ's Sacrifice. Actually, *"Faith vs. works"* has been the major dividing line between Catholics and Protestants for years. Catholics believe you must have faith and works to be saved, while Protestants believe Salvation is based on Faith alone — Faith in a Work already finished. *"When Jesus therefore had received the vinegar, He said,* **It is finished***: and He bowed His head, and gave up the ghost"* (Jn. 19:30).

GRACE

The Biblical Faith of which the Christian speaks is really **Faith in Grace.** In other words, it is by Grace that you are saved, and God's Grace is provided through Christ's Cross, the Cross itself being the ultimate manifestation of Grace. This is why the Object of your Faith must be Christ's Cross and Christ's Cross alone — because God's Grace flows from Christ's Cross and from Christ's Cross alone! It was God's Provision and His Plan before the Fall of man ever took place, *"Forasmuch as you know that you were not Redeemed with corruptible things, as silver and gold, from your vain conversation received by tradition from your fathers. But with the Precious Blood of Christ, as of a Lamb without blemish and without spot: Who verily was foreordained before the foundation of the world, but was manifest in these last times for you"* (I Pet. 1:18-20), so it is the only way to reach right relationship with the Father.

Furthermore, when the Catholic claims to put grace and works together, he does not realize that he has actually contradicted himself. **Grace and works are mutually exclusive concepts**; one automatically cancels out the other, so Faith in Grace cannot exist at the same time as faith in works. Author Dave Hunt says, *"Grace* *by its very nature excludes works. One cannot earn, merit, or pay for grace or else it would no longer be grace"* (A Woman Rides The Beast — p. 356).

You must choose one way, and the Bible is clearly on the side of Grace: *"For **by Grace are you saved through Faith**; and that not of yourselves: it is the Gift of God: **Not of works**, lest any man should boast"* (Eph. 2:8-9). You can no more have a half-grace than a half-truth, so if you choose Grace, you must lay down your works.

Unfortunately, modern evangelicals make the same mistake in logic when they claim to have a similar faith with Catholics; Grace and works don't mix. And the same choice applies to the Sanctification and/or growth of the Believer. He must either trust God's Grace or his own works for **all righteous living**, and upon making this choice, he must understand that Christ's Cross of Grace will never mix with man's cross of works. And a cross of works is not the Cross of Christ. *"**For I am not ashamed of the Gospel of Christ: for it is the Power of God unto Salvation to every one who believes; to the Jew first, and also to the Greek. For therein is the Righteousness of God revealed from faith to faith: as it is written, The just shall live by Faith"*** (Rom. 1:16-17).

I am not ashamed of the Gospel of Christ and Him Crucified; I am not ashamed of His Cross of Grace, Mercy, and Love. What an amazing blessing to know that we will never have to fail because God's Grace will never fail! We are justified *"from faith to faith,"* not from good work to good work. **Christ's Cross forever stands, so that we may live the Resurrection Life from grace to grace; this is the Power of God!** Oh praise the Lord, by Faith, our walk with Him is forever secured!

THE CATHOLIC UPDATE

Let's take a look at some material provided by one Catholic teacher from St. George Catholic School in Baton Rouge, LA, when a concerned parent asked this question: *". . . It would greatly further my understanding on the* **Catholic religion's point of view** *if you could answer a question for me. That question is, How do you, as a teacher of Catholicism, teach children or adults how to get to heaven? Or what is the plan of salvation?"* The teacher's reply included the following: *". . . Instead of trying to explain the Catholic point of view myself, I decided to send you a copy of a 'Catholic Update' which I recently read. I think this article is well written and will provide you with the information you seek. . . ."*

The *Catholic Update* is a widely read and well-respected magazine among Catholic families. It's publishing organization, St. Anthony Messenger Press, does its work with the official ecclesiastical approval of the Roman Catholic Archbishop of Cincinnati. This particular article of the *Catholic Update* was entitled *"What It Means to Be 'Saved,'"* but despite its lengthy analysis on the meaning of salvation, the Biblical salvation message was never clearly communicated. And furthermore, any half-way decipherable message in this vague philosophical manuscript can only be concluded to be completely Anti-Biblical.

Here are some of the main thoughts from this article that speak of salvation but never fully explain the truth of how one receives it: *". . . 'saved' means to be transformed by a loving God — from within ourselves and from within our most significant human relationships . . . small experiences of salvation happen in the fabric of everyday life . . . quietly saving moment . . . Some fundamentalist Christians believe that a person can be 'saved' in an instant . . . Catholics and many Protestants disagree. We are 'saved' now, but not entirely. We still must struggle with sin, with fear, with the dark side of human existence and the world. Salvation is a process, not a single event — a process that culminates only with eternal life . . . as far as God is concerned, we are saved: We need only to respond . . . Salvation, then, means that we are given the power to overcome sinful divisions, to be reconciled in our relationships with one another and with God. Healing and wholeness are God's gift to us for the asking . . . Christ's invitation to accept themselves as loved by God unconditionally, his call to give themselves in service to others. This embrace, Christians know, is the only rescue from darkness and death of all kinds, the only path to wellness and wholeness . . . one of the most personal ways we experience salvation is through liberation from fear and anxiety . . . this is the bottom line for a Christian's understanding of salvation . . . in a very real sense each person stands alone before God. That's one reason private prayers and occasional times of solitude are important to a Christian life. Today, however, for the sake of balance, we try to recover the scriptural perspective which attends to the social nature of salvation. It's not possible to be a Christian in private . . . Salvation's new life can come through political leaders from different religious and philosophical backgrounds who are in some way willing to trust in God's saving presence . . . more 'saved,' more whole. . . ."*

SALVATION WITHOUT FAITH IN CHRIST?

Did you hear any mention that one must admit to being a sinner, repent, and accept the Blood of Jesus to be saved in any of these peculiar definitions of salvation? And the dreadfully inaccurate explanations of salvation continue to get even worse: *"The Council said: 'Those also can attain to everlasting salvation who through no fault of their own do not know the gospel of Christ or his church, yet sincerely seek God and, moved by grace, strive by their deeds to do his will as it is known to them through the dictates of conscience . . . there is no dimension of human existence, no part of creation that is not subject to salvation, to healing, and wholeness. Human relationships, economic, philosophical and political systems, societies, individuals, human emotions and human institutions, technology, sickness and suffering, the natural environment, and the universe — all can be profoundly 'saved' by human openness to God's transforming inner presence. . . . 'Salvation' (like the words, 'healing,' 'making whole,' 'setting free' and 'restoring to right order' and 'wellness') is a bottomless word, meant to describe an overwhelming good, a good beyond human comprehension. The more we gaze into its depths, the more meanings it reveals . . . Perhaps Julian of Norwich,*

76 The Modern Babylon

a 13th-century English mystic and very practical person, best sums up the meaning of salvation. With the certainty of faith she writes that the fullness of life that we all hunger for and want to enjoy without end is a sure thing. Says she: 'All shall be well, and all shall be well, and all manner of things shall be well.' That's what salvation means."

REDEMPTION!

Again, I ask, where is the Gospel of Christ and Him Crucified that the Bible clearly explains is where one must exclusively place his Faith in order to be saved from sin? The article calls Jesus a savior several times but doesn't really explain how Jesus is Savior. At one point a *"Christ event"* (described as the life, death, and resurrection of Jesus) is mentioned, but even this description managed to avoid the clear salvation message. Regarding the *"Christ event,"* the article says that this event *". . . accomplished a fundamental shift in our relationship with God and our understanding of that relationship. Jesus showed the world how things really are between God and his creation, that the world, humankind, and all God's creation are being healed and made whole. The 'Christ event' revealed that human life and the cosmos are founded on Good, not evil, and that in the end death is a fall into the arms of Love."*

This is simply not true; the truth is that we are all *"dead in sin"* (Eph. 2:1, Col. 2:13) and cannot be made whole unless we are Redeemed by the Lord, and how can one be Redeemed unless someone tells him the **True Message** of Salvation? *"How then shall they call on Him in Whom they have not believed? and how shall they believe in Him of Whom they have not heard? and how shall they hear without a Preacher?"* (Rom. 10:14).

WHICH JESUS?

Any reference to Jesus Christ or His Gospel that does not deliberately and expressly communicate the Pure Gospel of Salvation is actually introducing you to another gospel and another Jesus — a false gospel and an Anti-Christ. And its messenger uses the Lord's name in vain. Jesus said: *"But let your communication be, Yes, yes; No, no: for whatsoever is more than these comes of evil"* (Mat. 5:37). If you have to guess at what the person believes, he is a false shepherd. It should be clear what a Christian believes and stands for, and while the CIA may have secret agents, God does not. The Holy Spirit will never hide the Truth of Salvation; nor will He speak it with compromising diplomacy. Salvation will not be a mystery when the Lord is leading the messenger. *"No man, when he has lit a candle, puts it in a secret place, neither under a bushel, but on a candlestick, that they which come in may see the light"* (Lk. 11:33).

So when any messenger, including America's favorite preacher, (and other unexpected messengers like a *"Christian"* movie/entertainment, a politician, an angel, or even an alien) comes claiming Christ, no matter how kind and sincere he may be, you should immediately judge the *"Jesus"* he presents. What *"Christ"* does he serve? Is it the *"Christ"* of the Cross? A *"Christ"* of good works? And just because you judge a man's gospel, does not mean you are guilty of judging the man. *"But **though we, or an Angel** from Heaven, Preach **any other gospel** unto you than that which we have preached unto you, let him be accursed"* (Gal. 1:8). *"For if he that comes Preaching **another Jesus**, whom we have not Preached, or if you receive another spirit, which you have not received, or **another gospel**, which you have not accepted, you might well bear with him"* (II Cor. 11:4). *"And He said, **Take heed that you be not deceived: for many shall come in My Name**, saying, I am Christ; and the time draws near: go you not therefore after them"* (Lk. 21:8).

GOOD INTENTIONS?

However, the *Catholic Update* article, in fact, states that one may be saved **without knowing the Gospel of Christ at all**, just so long as he has *"good"* intentions for life, living, and the pursuit of God. It is amazing that even our good intentions seem good enough to us to merit our salvation, and if we are gut-wrenchingly honest, we really believe that our good intentions should be allowed to save us. Why? — because we actually think they are good. You see, deep down we disagree with God in regard to our own goodness. Our sin is so far beyond our own belief that our pride will not let us believe it, and we spend the majority of our time totally oblivious to it.

But the Bible says, *"**The heart is deceitful** above all things, and desperately wicked: who can know it?"* (Jer. 17:9). This is why it takes a Miracle of God for someone to have a True Born-Again Salvation Experience. God's Word and the convicting Power of the Holy Spirit have to brake through our delusion, so for the first time, a person can say, *"God, I don't know, but You do know . . . it is not what I think, but what You think . . . and You say that not only am I sinful, I cannot merit my own salvation. . . ."* And in acknowledging that God's ways are higher than his own, he has finally humbled himself before an Almighty God. And when a person accepts the truth of his own evil nature, he is more likely to seek God's Mercy rather than trying to convince himself and others that he is *"good."*

This, in turn, leads to the Cross. In this sense, obvious sins could be a blessing in disguise; they could make it easier for a man to see his unworthiness, and it is only in recognizing such that he may be truly blessed.

So, I think it is safe to say that the most deceptive kind of false gospel is one that relies on the *"goodness"* of man. While our **works often make us feel worthy, clean, and religiously acceptable**, the Lord is actually repulsed and sickened by them when they divert people from His Gospel of Grace. *"But we are all as an **unclean** thing, and all **our righteousnesses are as filthy rags**; and we all do fade as a leaf; and our iniquities, like the wind, have taken us away"* (Isa. 64:6).

CHAPTER EIGHT

ASSURANCE OF SALVATION?

Another tragic consequence of the Catholic false way of works salvation is that the Believer is never completely assured of his salvation; he must even endure purgatory before he can attain complete salvation and enter Heaven. In fact, any Catholic that claims assurance of his salvation is actually put out of the church. *"If anyone says that in order to obtain the remission of sins it is necessary . . . to believe with certainty and without hesitation . . . that his sins are forgiven him, let him be anathema"* (Council of Trent, Six, XVI, 13). This is a burden that the Lord never intended, and it explains why the Catholic feels such a strong compulsion to follow the Roman Church and its traditions. This is exactly what the Roman Catholic Church wants.

According to Vatican Council II, at least some of the *"saving"* works should be directly performed through the institutional church: *"For it is the liturgy through which, especially in the divine sacrifice of the Eucharist, the work of redemption is accomplished. . . ."* The church today echoes with eerily similar statements like, *"A church family identifies you as a genuine believer"* (Rick Warren, *The Purpose Driven Life*, p. 133).

As the Catholic Church emphasizes *"saving"* action through the church, the modern church says that active church involvement is verification of authentic salvation. Both try to institutionalize salvation. By nature, this way is a form of manipulation used to control the laity which the Lord has called the *"doctrine of the Nicolaitanes"* and said He hated: *"So have you also them who hold the doctrine of the Nicolaitanes, which thing I hate"* (Rev. 2:15).

The true Biblical way of Salvation, on the other hand, provides

80 *The Modern Babylon*

an ever-present **witness of the Holy Spirit** to the individual that he is saved. Did you hear that? God Himself provides assurance to His Children, so that no man's religious witness or church government should be able to control them. It is upon belief in one's desperate state of sinfulness and the need of the saving work of Jesus, that one's soul can be instantly ripped from the grasp of Satan and placed into the hand of the Lord. *"The Spirit itself bears witness with our spirit, that we are the Children of God"* (Rom. 8:16).

PROCESS THEOLOGY

Salvation is a *"change,"* not a gradual process of *"changing"* because the only possible provision for *"the change"* was already made at a specified point in time, long ago at Calvary's Cross! The idea of ***"Process Theology"*** actually has roots from a Grecian philosopher named Heraclites who viewed reality in terms of *"becoming"* rather than *"being."* Heraclites claimed that *". . . the basis of reality was change and flux."*

In past times, Catholics have primarily focused on the traditional *"saving works"* of the sacraments, the most important being the Mass, which perfectly demonstrates the **theology of** *"process salvation"* itself. The Mass constitutes the perpetual **re-sacrificing of Christ** as provision for the perpetual *"process"* the individual must embrace. In other words, the Mass is the provision for a *"process,"* while the Cross was the provision for a completed rebirth. The re-killing of Christ in the Mass (since the Catholic Church teaches that the bread and wine turn into the literal Body and Blood of Christ, a.k.a. *"transubstantiation"*) is a horrific work that the Catholic would not feel necessary to repeat if he believed that Faith in Jesus' one-time Sacrifice had been sufficient.

Today, the definition of the sacraments and other *"saving works"* are being enlarged. With the same compromising spirit used to increase its numbers and allegiances in the past, the Catholic Church's expansion of *"saving works"* now include basically any good deed — just as long as the action brings **positively good** things to oneself or other people.

CHANGE AGENTS

And, once again, the leading Catholic "***change agents***" are playing games with words to bring today's **neo-pagans** into their ranks. Such **stealth lingos** always have positive-sounding meaning to those who do not have **initiation rights** to the real meanings, and this time around, the salvation process is described in **New Age terminology** — a terminology so obscurely defined and inoffensive it could be used to combine almost any varying theologies, even humanistic philosophies and sciences.

For example, some terms that are being substituted for "*salvation*" and used to alter its meaning include "*wholeness,*" "*wellness,*" "*healing,*" "*actualization,*" "*transcendence*" and "*transformation.*" Even secular society wants to "*heal the world.*"

One well-known Catholic mystic, Teilhard de Chardin, has said: "*. . . the Cross still stands . . . But this is on one condition, and one only: that it expand itself to the dimensions of a New Age, and cease to present itself to us as primarily (or even exclusively) the sign of a victory over sin. . . .*" Furthermore, he called the "*religion of the future*" a "***religion of evolution***," evolution itself being precisely "*a process of change.*"

As we saw, the *Catholic Update* has described salvation as the **growth process** of "***working*** *through human decisions, actions and relationships, leading individuals, families, communities, and societies to* ***wholeness***." See, Catholic "*salvation,*" in addition to being a process, is considered to be both collective and individual, a "*universal*" work. New-agers find common ground in this "*universal*" work, calling it a "*cosmic evolution*" — the next stage of humanity's evolution involving a **leap into the spiritual realm**. Even many in the Protestant church world are speaking of a new "***transformation**" in which various "*transformative activities*" help renew the world in preparation of Christ's return and are considered indicators of "*revival.*"

It is scary to learn, as well, that new-age leaders who have infiltrated the secular education system have cunningly termed this same **mind-set of redemption** *"higher order thinking skills,"* indicating that it is a more advanced, a more intelligent way to think, when it is really just a different way to process information (actually part of the *"dumbing down"* report of modern education) according to man-made **ethical principles**, principles that can and will be **modified by consensus** on a regular basis. Thereby, there can never be any factual absolutes, just moral relativities. The overall idea is that all of humanity and the universe (although adherence is chosen on an individual basis) can work together in this evolutionary process of being saved and made whole as **heroes and saints on earth**, changing the world from a *"fallen"* condition to a *"redeemed"* condition just as the *"patron saints"* have been helping redeem the world (*"co-redeeming"*) from their cosmological positions for decades.

Mother Teresa would be one such modern-day hero (of course, Gandhi, the Hindu peace advocate, would be no different). Just think about it, the predominant Catholic *"witness"* for many years has been its *"good works"* not its evangelical preaching. It is also a well-established Catholic teaching that Mary, the mother of Christ, has been called a *"Co-Redemptrix"* for centuries, and now, in the newly **emerging church of Babylon**, we are all considered **co-redeemers** together with Christ. So, just as the idol *"saints"* were previously heroes on earth, every person should strive for this same heroic status to help save mankind.

NEW AGE

The New Age Journal reported of one so-called *"**Planetary Mass**"* that celebrated the Earth and coming of the *"cosmic Christ."* It was held in San Francisco's Grace Episcopal Cathedral (termed *"a mainstream Christian denomination"*) in which the New Age reporter partook of the Mass as *"the body of Christ,"* but in its expanded understanding as *"... part of the divine Body of the universe ... the energy of the 'cosmic Christ.'"* Another interesting twist to this story is that this New-Age reporter is also an ex-Catholic whose personal reflection of the event included the following: *"Had there been a Planetary Mass in my parish twenty-five years ago, I realized, I might never have left the Church."* So, a New-ager found spiritual fulfillment within the revised all-inclusive Catholic Mass. And as a few have wisely discovered, **the *"process"* itself is the greatest idol of all** because the *"process of salvation"* is quickly becoming the new *"Christ"* of salvation. But, **Jesus Christ is not a process, He is a person**.

Anything that separates you from the Person and Office of Jesus Christ, and what He did at the Cross, is a false way of salvation and cannot save you. Jesus Christ is the Source of salvation, not a process called *"Christ."* And neither can you call Him a philosophy, a *"new way of thinking"*, a *"new level of consciousness"*, or a *"Christ-consciousness,"* the preferred term of the New Age. Jesus Christ came to Earth as a specified person, the historical man from Galilee. *"For many deceivers are entered into the world, who confess not that Jesus Christ is come **in the flesh**. This is a deceiver and an Antichrist"* (II Jn. 1:7). You must come out of your *"saving processes"* of believing, thinking, or doing and into the Person of Christ, the only Way of Righteousness.

Your works will fail anyway as you discover that you cannot **consciously** learn to choose good over evil. This *"Christ philosophy"* is an integral part of the **Roman system** that **separates people from Jesus**, and even if one never bears the name, Roman Catholic, the Lord said that when one joins himself to a harlot, he becomes one with her. *". . . Do you not know that he which is **joined to an harlot** is one body? for two, said He, shall be one flesh"* (I Cor. 6:16). And to those who may not join but would refuse to stand against Rome the Lord has this to say: *". . . Whosoever transgresses, and abides not in the Doctrine of Christ, has not God. He who abides in the Doctrine of Christ, he has Both the Father and the Son. If there come any unto you, and bring not this Doctrine, receive him not into your house, neither bid him God speed: For **he that bids him God speed is partaker** of his evil deeds"* (II Jn. 1: 9-11).

WHAT FELLOWSHIP DOES LIGHT HAVE WITH DARKNESS?

What is the opposite of Grace? — works. What is the opposite of a wicked heart? — a good heart. What is the opposite of a completed Sacrifice on the Cross? — a perpetually incomplete sacrifice. How can directly opposite views be reconciled? The Word of God asks, *"What fellowship does light have with darkness?"* (II Cor. 6:14). Catholicism and Biblical Christianity are directly opposing, opposite ideologies, so trying to find commonalities between the two has gone far beyond stupidity. It is what you call deception! The Evangelical Church today is deceived when it signs alliances of faith with the Roman Catholic Church. It has become a coward and a traitor to the Faith, the Pure Gospel of Jesus Christ — the one Truth it was called to defend!

Following the Catholic concept of *"process salvation"* throughout which a poor soul never experiences the full security of his salvation until after the gates of Heaven have been securely shut behind him, neither does a faithful Catholic have any guarantee of when he will be allowed to enter those Pearly Gates even after his death. As we have mentioned, Catholicism teaches that after death, the soul must first go to a place called *"purgatory"* where they have to endure some **purging**, some unknown amount of **suffering** and **pain** to be made completely *"fit"* for Heaven.

What a tragic and oppressive religion to follow! How does the Believer bear the thought of the coming torments? Certainly, he would do everything possible in this life to *"pay his due"* and shorten this prison time in the afterlife. You see, Catholicism teaches that while the guilt of sin could be removed by Christ's Sacrifice, further suffering was needed to actually **cleanse** and **purify** the Believer from sin. Apparently, according to Catholicism, Christ didn't quite pay it all!

So, before we dismiss purgatorial suffering as a minor theological debate, we should recognize that belief in this concept puts one in a position that denies the Blood of the Lamb! The doctrine of purgatory is a targeted attack and direct hit at the heart of the Gospel. Scripture expresses only one object that cleanses from all sin — **Jesus and His Blood (Christ's death on the Cross)**. And when Christ's Work on the Cross was completed, the terms for all future cleansing were complete as well. *". . . The Blood of Jesus Christ, His Son, **cleanses us from all sin**"* (I Jn. 1:7). *". . . When he had **by Himself purged our sins**, sat down on the Right Hand of the Majesty on high"* (Heb. 1:3).

SUFFERING?

The theme of *"suffering"* is actually found throughout Catholic tradition in its **ascetic concepts** which teach one to deny material pleasure for Spiritual Growth. Some forms have included fasting, celibacy, and frugal living, but the *"sufferings"* have also been quite serious. In the past, some groups of Catholics practiced public **flagellation as penance**. And even stranger forms of suffering like *"stigmata"* have appeared in Catholic circles as well. You got it: *"no pain, no gain."* And isn't this precisely the same system the world follows? It actually appeals to man's pride of life.

Pain, used in this sense, is a form of earning something; it is a form of merit. But the Bible never taught us that we can achieve Salvation by following a strict diet and exercise program. The Bible teaches that Salvation comes from Christ's sufferings, not our own. It is His pain from which we benefit: *"That I may know Him, and the power of His Resurrection, and the fellowship of **His sufferings**, being made conformable unto His death"* (Phil. 3:10).

So, again we see the process of *"works"* emerge from the Roman Catholic Church. This **works-mentality** is often difficult to recognize as Satan has done a good job preconditioning our minds to it. See, all systems of the world (including false religious notions like *"karma"*) have taught us that we get what we deserve. But, Glory to God; it is the true Gospel of Jesus Christ that gives us a **whole new thing**! *"How long will you go about, O thou backsliding daughter? for the LORD hath created **a new thing in the Earth**, A woman shall compass a man"* (Jer. 31:22). Jesus Christ gives

Salvation, Grace, and Mercy to the believing sinner even though he doesn't deserve it. Again, Christianity is not a *"works"* salvation! We cling to the Cross!

Unfortunately, the Catholic Church remains insistent upon its *"sufferings,"* in which purgatory tops the list. Catholic sympathizer, C.S. Lewis, ironically heralded as one of Christianity's most brilliant defenders of the faith, may have said it best when he described purgatory as just a continuation of the salvation process. In the *Letter of C.S. Lewis* (p.246-247), speaking of purgatory, Lewis says it is *"a process by which the **work of redemption continues**, and first perhaps begins to be noticeable after death."* C.S. Lewis has also stated in *Letters to Malcolm: Chiefly on Prayer*: *"I believe in Purgatory . . . souls demand Purgatory"* (p.108-109).

But, belief in purgatory is almost incomprehensible considering it was taught neither by Jesus, nor His Disciples, nor the Early Church of the New Testament. Furthermore, there is not one single reference or anything alluding to it anywhere in the Bible! All notions of *"purgatory"* (or prayers for the souls trapped in it) were unheard of in the professing church even to the slightest degree until A.D. 600, when Pope Gregory the Great made claims about a *"third"* state — a place for purification of the soul before its entrance into Heaven. Even this concept was not accepted as a dogma of the Catholic Church until the council of Florence in 1459; it was ninety years later that the Council of Trent confirmed the teaching, cursing those who would not accept it.

CHAPTER NINE

Interestingly, during the Twelfth Century, a **legend** was conveniently spread to help bring the fictitious *"purgatory"* to life. And what better promotes a lie than an **enchanting story** to go along with it? Even today, this method is employed by many in the modern *"church"* who try to promote false versions of Christianity.

As this particular tale goes, St. Patrick claimed he had found the entrance to purgatory. He even had an exceptionally deep pit dug in Ireland in order to convince any **unimaginative** doubters. Several **monks** claimed they descended into the pit, and of course, upon their return, they could vividly describe both Hell and purgatory. Coming from these *"church"* **leaders**, the **testimonies** of such **experiences** were certainly persuasive. In 1153, an Irish knight (a *"knight"* being another respected and trusted citizen of that time) named Owen also claimed that he had descended into the pit, and the account of his nether experience helped persuade remaining skeptics as well.

So, St. Patrick's *"pit"* became a box-office hit as the masses came from afar to visit the infamous entrance to purgatory. However, to those who held to the **truth of Scripture** rather than putting stock in the **chronicles of men**, it was not surprising that St. Patrick's *"pit"* was later ordered to be closed as a fraud in 1497. In fact, the abuses of finance surrounding this **mystical tourist attraction** forced Pope Alexander VI to close it.

Amazingly, a mere three years later in Rome, Pope Benedict XIV was still able to preach and publish a sermon in favor of St. Patrick's purgatory. Something about a story really grips the soul; it is sad that many, many ridiculous tales of the afterlife and other subjects of faith flourished during this time. Many of these fabrications became an integral part of **Catholic tradition**, being passed on from generation to generation. *"The words of a talebearer are as wounds, and they go down into the innermost parts of the belly"* (Prov. 18:8).

MONEY!

Why would the Catholic Church care so much about these tales and traditions? Because *". . . the love of money is the root of all evil . . ."* (I Tim. 6:10), and such stories help install the fear and pressure necessary to swindle the **Biblically uneducated** masses out of every penny. *"Purgatory"* has undoubtedly provided the Catholic Church with a very effectual means to rake heaping piles of money into its coffers.

This *"church"* actually has the nerve to demand a fee from a member who needs a priest to *"pray a loved one out of purgatory."* And faithful followers actually obey, even when the priests themselves admit they have no way of knowing for sure when a soul has passed from purgatory to Heaven. The very idea that we can assure salvation with money is utterly heathenistic, as we will see, but who wouldn't pay a fee to make sure a friend or family member made it to Heaven? Is it any wonder that Catholics will give all they have considering that they have been taught since childhood that priests can pray their loved ones out of the burning flames?

A doctrine like this is wicked and cruel; it is worse than any system of gambling, fraud, or the conspiring of common thieves. To play upon the tender memories of hurting people and cheat them out of their hard earned wages is a heartless thing to do in the name of God. Yet, it is through various types of financial scandal that the Catholic Church has gained much of its vast riches; today, the wealth of the Vatican is said to be immeasurable.

The Catholic Church mercilessly tells even poor widow women they need to pay for their deceased husbands to be prayed out of purgatory when the Lord had condemned this practice specifically: *"Woe unto you, Scribes and Pharisees, hypocrites! for you **devour widows' houses, and for a pretence make long prayer: therefore*** *you shall receive the greater damnation"* (Mat. 23:14).

If a priest really has the power to pray a deceased soul into Heaven, shouldn't his prayers be free? If priests really love God and the Catholic Church really is *"the One and Only"* Church, why are they so greedy as to **charge money for ministry**?

Catholic masses can be bought for a price as well, and are an integral part of prayers for the dead in purgatory. A high mass (sung with loud voices), is one of great significance possibly costing one thousand dollars or more, depending on the amount of added benefits like flowers, candles, or priestly intercession during the ceremony. A low mass of less importance (performed using lowered voices) is less expensive and usually contains only six candles. In other words: High money, high mass — low money, low mass — no money, no mass!

On the contrary, God does not show this type of favoritism: *". . . God is no respecter of persons"* (Acts 10:34). Souls whose living relatives simply can't afford, or refuse, to pay for masses are called the *"forgotten souls in purgatory."* So, on November 2nd (known as *"All Soul's Day"*), prayers are said for them. A fervent plea is made to all members of the Catholic Church to contribute money to the *"Requiem Mass,"* the mass said on this day for those unfortunate souls with pitiless relatives. How desperate and guilty one must feel who cannot afford a mass for his relatives!

PURGATORIAL SOCIETY?

Some Catholics have found an alternative to secure their eventual deliverance from the purgatorial fires in joining the Purgatorial Society established in 1856; they make contributions to this fund to assure that, upon death, there will be prayers said for them. But Scripture makes it clear that it is impossible to redeem a man's soul with money! The Bible could not be any plainer on this issue: *"Forasmuch as you know that you were **not Redeemed with corruptible things**, as silver and gold, from your **vain conversation received by tradition** from your fathers; But with the Precious Blood of Christ,* *as of a Lamb without blemish and without spot"* (I Pet. 1:18-19).

Teaching that money can buy the blessings and gifts of God, much less redeem a soul, is blatant mockery to the Blood of Christ! Certainly then, even if *"purgatory"* did exist, money could never free anyone from it! *"But Peter said unto him,* **Your money perish with you, because you have thought that the Gift of God may be purchased with money***"* (Acts 8:20).

It makes perfect sense, as well, to see that paying money to benefit the dead actually originated in paganism. The Lord had clearly forbidden it as He did not want His people mixing pagan concepts with their worship of Him. *"I have not eaten thereof in my mourning, neither have I taken away ought thereof for any unclean use, nor given ought thereof for the dead: but I have hearkened to the voice of the LORD my God, and have done according to all that you have commanded me"* (Deut. 26:14). Dependence on money is denial of the Cross!

CHRIST AND HIM CRUCIFIED

Unredeemed man incessantly, although erroneously, believes that, if he keeps seeking, his discoveries will ultimately bring the revelation that will solve the problems of society, but it is only the One Revelation of Christ and Him Crucified that addressed the circumstances of the Fall. What's more, God's Wisdom tells us that no philosophy birthed by man will ever be completely original. *"The thing that has been, it is that which shall be; and that which is done is that which shall be done: and there is* **no new thing under the sun***. Is there any thing whereof it may be said, See, this is new? it hath been already of old time, which was before us. There is no remembrance of former things; neither shall there be any remembrance of things that are to come with those that shall come after"* (Eccl. 1:9-11). So, since *"purgatory"* contradicts the Revelation of Christ's Cross, there is a good chance its concepts were taught some time in the past.

Sure enough, the true origin of *"purgatory"* is easily found within ancient paganism, long before the Christian era. And, as well, traces of *"purgatory," "purifying fires,"* and/or *"prayers for the dead"* are found in nearly every system of the world — both religious and secular. Even in the mystery religion of Egypt, it was believed that priestly intervention was necessary for prayers to the dead to be effectual.

Take the famous Greek philosopher, Plato, he lived from 427 to 347 B.C. and spoke of the Orphis teachers of his day *"who flock to the rich man's doors, and try to persuade him that they have **power at their command**, which they procure from Heaven, which enables them by sacrifices and incantation — to make amends for any crime committed by the individual himself or his ancestors.* ***Their mysteries deliver us from the torments of the other world****, while the neglect of them is punished by an awful doom."*

Talk about a **white magic** ceremony! No matter what religious professional title you hold — whether, preacher, teacher, prophet, priest, etc. — attempting to **command the heavenly realm** through **mystical sacraments**, rites, or rituals (like the sacrifice of the mass) makes you a **sorcerer**, not a minister!

PAGANISM

One can find an elaborate description of purgatorial suffering in the sacred writings of Buddhism as well. The Chinese Buddhists came to buy prayers for loved ones in purgatory so often that shops were set up specifically for this purpose.

Hinduism also teaches its followers about realms of Hell that are not final dwelling places for souls. Sinful people are just punished and suffer in these realms for a certain amount of time. When the time is up, the sinner is released to participate in the **cycle of reincarnation**.

In the religion of Zoroastrianism, (religion of the Persian Empire) souls had to endure twelve stages of suffering before they could be sufficiently purified to enter Heaven. Occult knowledge says that the number twelve indicates a completed **cycle of cosmic** order, in which **consciousness of a new reality** may occur.

The Stoics believed in a middle place of *"**enlightenment**"* which they called *"Empurosis,"* meaning *"a place of fire."* *"Enlightenment"* can also connect with occult knowledge when it refers to the forbidden secrets of the **Tree of the Knowledge of Good and Evil**.

The Celtic Fire Goddess, Brigid, is celebrated in the fire-festival called, Imbolc, held in February; *"Februum"* is a Latin word meaning *"purification."* The Celts celebrate Brigid's *"purifying fires"* in this month.

Islamic teaching also includes ideas similar to purgatory. Like many religions, different Muslim sects have varying ideas, but we do find purgatorial concepts amid their doctrine. Most Islamic tradition teaches that after death the soul must enter a place of limbo called the *"grave"* until the Day of the Resurrection in which all spirits will receive their last judgment, sending them to their eternal home. Theologians of the Muslim Asharite School say that, in the *"grave,"* Allah can *"forgive his sins or nonconformities and remove him, either immediately or after a certain period during which imperfections had been 'burned away.'"* They base this analysis on the following statement from the Hadith: *"He shall make men come out of hell after they have been burned and reduced to cinders."* Some Muslim theologians have also explained that, while the torment of the grave for the unbeliever is just a precursor to the everlasting suffering they will experience in Hell, the suffering a believer may have to endure is designed to purge the soul from lingering sin.

BABYLON

So, where did *"purgatorial"* concepts first originate? Again, we can return to ancient Babylon and the worship of the sun-god, Nimrod. **Fire** (as well as light) was viewed as the earthly representation of the **sun-god** and his **burning rays**. The name *"Tammuz"* (supposedly Nimrod **reincarnated**) has a very significant meaning regarding this fire-worship as well: it means *"to make perfect (Tam)* *by fire (Muz),*" signifying "*Fire the perfecter*" or "*the perfecting fire.*" So, the very name of the sun-god (in his second life form) proclaims that the perfection required for liberation and rebirth comes through his fire.

The Celtic tradition taught that fire (being the source of the light and warmth required for growth) is the element that gives humans the "***spark of life***" within.

Other false gods throughout history have proclaimed the redemptive power of fire as well. Dionysus (Greek) and/or Bacchus (Roman) was called "***fire-born.***" According to his legend, he was consumed in his father's flames, along with his mother, but was later rescued from them by his father (Zeus, Dionysus' father, initially struck him with a lightening bolt according to some versions of the story). Then, Zeus impregnated a mortal woman with Dionysus' **heart** (the only part of him not consumed) to be **reborn**. This explains why Dionysus was also called "***twice born.***"

Similarly, the Persian name, Zoroaster, comes from "*Zero-ashta,*" meaning "*seed of fire.*" According to Zoroastrian teaching, the father-fire god perfected all things and amassed them into his reincarnated form, specifically the "*second mind, whom all nations of men call the first,*" which replaced his worship as a father-figure (this "*second mind*" is also a picture of Nimrod as the child, Tammuz).

So, there seems to be at least two reoccurring patterns regarding the power of the Babylonian sun-god's fire — the purging of sin and the generation of new life.

FREEMASONRY

Interestingly, this exact terminology is used in *Morals and Dogmas of the Ancient and Accepted Scottish Rite of Freemasonry* by Albert Pike speaking of the father-fire god: "*All things are the progeny of one fire. The Father perfected all things and delivered them over to the Second mind, whom all nations of men call the First*" (p.447).

These traditions and lies mock and twist the description of Jesus Christ in the following Scripture: *"For whom He did foreknow, He also did predestinate to be conformed to the Image of His Son, that He might be the **firstborn** among many Brethren"* (Rom. 8:29). The true interpretation of this verse refers to Christ's foundation of Redemption completed at the Cross.

In fact, virtually every pagan religion believes in a god that died and was resurrected in some form or fashion. Often he was a repeated sacrifice, a perpetual *"**dying-and-rising**"* **god** who often reappeared in different forms. Actually, the original pagan intent of the *"yule log"* was to depict the resurrection of this god. The *"log"* (symbolizing the sun-god) was burned (sacrificed) on Christmas Eve and resurrected on Christmas Day in the form of the Christmas Tree.

There is even evidence of an ancient Egyptian Passion play depicting the death and resurrection of the sun-god, the king-divinity, Osiris. This annual drama kept the sufferings and triumph of this god afresh in the minds of the people.

This mimics the death, burial, and Resurrection of the True Lord and Savior Jesus Christ. So, here we see, yet another instance where Tammuz is portrayed as a false Christ figure.

THE JESUS DIED SPIRITUALLY DOCTRINE

Even more alarming, we see that this aspect of Tammuz has actually tiptoed its way into a sleeping modern *"church"* by way of the *"Jesus **died spiritually** doctrine,"* spread by Word of Faith teachers. The *"Jesus died spiritually doctrine"* teaches that Christ became a sinner on the cross (*"died spiritually"*) and subsequently went to Hell to complete the penalty for sin. After he had suffered all the torments of the burning side of Hell for three days and three nights, the Lord said, *"it is enough."* Jesus was then *"born-again"* (given new spiritual life) and resurrected from the dead. Indeed, Romans 8:29 is violated again as the Word of Faith proponents proclaim that this is where Christ became the *"firstborn,"* having been "***born-again***" just as any other sinner.

Here, we can also see the connection to the Catholic doctrine of process salvation. See, the actual **point of salvation** (the completed born-again experience) for a soul, according to Roman Catholic doctrine, is at the completion of their sufferings in purgatory. Catholic souls must suffer the burning flames before their salvation process can be complete, very similar to the *"Jesus died spiritually"* teaching that Christ had to suffer in Hell prior to his purported, yet completely fabricated, *"born-again"* experience.

Jesus was the sinless, spotless, Lamb of God, who never needed spiritual redemption. How could He? He is God; He is "***Jesus Christ the same yesterday, and today, and forever***" (Heb. 13:8). His Body of flesh was offered for us because we were the ones dead spiritually. We needed a Savior, not a tragic hero!

Astonishingly, this is another principle as found in Masonic doctrine: *"Christ completed the Atonement on the Cross by descending into Hell."* (Morals and Dogmas of the Ancient and Accepted Scottish Rite of Freemasonry, p.306) All these lies culminate into a false *"born-again"* experience that is not *"Christian"*! *"Born-again"* in Christ Jesus is not the same as *"reborn by fire."*

NIMROD

Now, Nimrod was known by yet another name — Molech (called by the names Mithras, Baal/Bel, Osiris, etc. as well). The Bible specifically speaks of the worship of Molech and the **dark rituals** involved in his worship. In the most fundamental descriptions of Molech-worship we find the notions of *"purifying fire."* Molech was, in fact, known as a fire-god, and it seems that the various pagan nations felt that his fire was necessary to cleanse one from sin as well.

Ceremonial rites in connection with Molech were brutally wicked; he was honored with **human sacrifice**, mutilation, vows of celibacy/virginity, and devotion to the firstborn. He was often represented in the form of a horrible idol with blazing fires inside his constructed figure. Sacrifices were placed in the fires of these idols to be consumed by the dreaded Molech all while **drums beat**, bands played, and **priests chanted**. Pagan priests would take babies straight from their mothers' arms to be sacrificed as the **dissonant sounds of pagan worship** drowned the agonizing screams. The Bible speaks of a valley called Topheth where such sacrifices were made. *"And he defiled Topheth . . ."* (II Ki. 23:10).

Correspondingly, other pagan religions have practiced these sacrifices. The Aztecs/Mayans of Mexico practiced human sacrifice, particularly by offering a victim's heart to the sun-god, Kukulcan/Quetzalcoatl. Undeniably, purgatory's purifying fires had a history among these cold-blooded **cleansing sacrifices** that God condemned. It was the belief in the cleansing powers of the sun that were behind the abominable rites of passing through the Satanic fires of Molech, and the Lord specifically warned: *". . . You shall not let any of your seed pass through the fire to Molech . . ."* (Lev. 18:21; II Ki. 23:10; Jer. 32:35).

Long ago the original pieces of *"purgatory"* had been scattered throughout the nations along with the rest of the scrap metal from Babylon's tower. And, yes, the pieces have settled and remain a part of the Roman Catholic Church even today, making it the perfect model for the Apocalyptic Apostate Church, the *"church"* who worships the false Christ of Babylon.

CHAPTER TEN

THE MOTHER AND THE CHILD

Another proof, unmatched among all scholarly evidence, that Babylonian pagan idolatry has continued, can be seen in the way the Roman Catholic Church inaugurated Mary-worship as its stand-in for the worship of the ancient Mother Goddess of Babylon — Queen Semiramis. After giving birth to Tammuz, she taught that he was a god-child (Nimrod re-born) and that he had been supernaturally conceived. Therefore, she, as both his mother and a virgin, was divine as well. And since this story was widely circulated throughout ancient Babylon, it developed into a well-established subject of worship — the worship of The Mother and The Child (subsequently, the Catholic "**Madonna and Child**").

This **image of The Mother and Child** was spread with the Babylonians as they were scattered to various parts of the Earth. Consequently, all nations in ancient times came to worship some form of this image centuries before the true Savior, Jesus, was ever born. Countless examples include the following. In India, she was called "*Indrani*" or "*Devaki*" and portrayed with a child, "*Krishna*," in her arms. For ages, they were also known as "*Isi*," the Great Goddess, and her child, "*Iswara*," and had great temples built in India for the purpose of their worship. She was "*Aphrodite*" or "*Ceres*" to the Greeks, "*Nana*" to the Sumerians, and "*Venus*" or "*Fortuna*" and her child called "*Jupiter*" to her Roman followers. In Asia, the "*Mother*" was known as "*Cybele*" and the child as "*Deoius*." The ancient Germans worshipped the virgin "*Hertha*," complete with a child in her arms. The Scandinavians called her "*Disa*," who was also pictured with child. The Etruscans called her "*Nutria*." The worship of the Mother and Child was even known in old England; in 1747, a religious monument of pagan origin was found in Oxford exhibiting a female nursing an infant.

Among the Chinese, the Mother Goddess was called *"Shing Moo"* or the *"Holy Mother."* Again, she is pictured with the child in her arms and rays of glory around her head. These *"rays of glory,"* show the connection to the Babylonian sun-god just as many examples of such **sun imagery in Catholic art**. One missionary to China, Dr. Gutzlaff, concluded that *"Shing Moo"* must have surely been borrowed from the Roman Church; he also felt that her character was clear evidence of paganism and Catholicism's integration.

In Egypt, the Mother Goddess was known as *"Isis"* and her child *"Horus"* or *"Osiris"* (as the father-figure); it is common to see drawings of *"Isis"* with *"Horus"* seated in her lap among religious monuments of Egypt. *"Isis"* was actually known as the goddess of fertility and became an archetype for a sort-of feminine life force. The Egyptians considered *"Isis"* to be the essence of the feminine energy within every person, also called the *"yin"* **principle** in Chinese philosophy.

In fact, the original character of I-Ching depicts both the male (a.k.a. **the sun** or *"yang"* principle) and the female (a.k.a. **the moon** or *"yin"* principle). How many psychiatrists today advise men to get in touch with their feminine side? Trendy *"Christian"* books now suggest that the female temperament is the part of *"God's image"* a woman was always meant to reflect.

Likewise, many other religious seekers are looking for the light of the goddess that will soon reveal her hidden truths to humanity. Indeed, the *"woman"* of Babylon is emerging, and this *"Madonna"* will shine brighter than her secular shadow, pop-singer Madonna, ever dreamed possible.

THE QUEEN OF HEAVEN

The Goddess was also known as *"Stella Maris,"* or *"Star of the Sea."* This title directly connects to the title given to the Catholic version of Mary as **"St. Mary, Star of the Sea"** or **"Lady of the**

Lake." Many Catholic-based hospitals make use of such titles, alluding to the source from which they believe healing actually comes. You see, healing power was attributed to the pagan Mother Goddess as well. Arthurian legends alluded to her as the "*lady of the lake*" who held the magical Excalibur sword out of the water that healed the wounded king. This should make the waters crystal clear — the Catholic version of Mary is really the ancient Goddess of Babylon, not the Mary of the Bible.

Sadly, even the children of Israel were defiled by this Mother Goddess worship when they fell into apostasy: "*And they forsook the LORD, and served Baal and Ashtaroth*" (Judg. 2:13) — "*Ashtaroth*" (a.k.a. "*Ashtar*" and "*Ishtar*") being the name by which the goddess was known to the children of Israel. Another title by which the goddess was known among the Israelites was "***The Queen of Heaven.***" "*But we will certainly do whatsoever thing goeth forth out of our own mouth, to **burn incense** unto the Queen of Heaven, and to pour out **drink offerings** unto her, as we have done, we, and our fathers, our kings, and our princes, in the cities of Judah, and in the streets of Jerusalem: for then had we plenty of victuals, and were well, and saw no evil. But since we left off to burn incense to the Queen of Heaven, and to pour out drink offerings unto her, we have wanted all things, and have been consumed by the sword and by the famine. And when we burned incense to the Queen of Heaven, and poured out drink offerings unto her, did we make her **cakes** to worship her, and pour out drink offerings unto her, without our men*" (Jer. 44:17-19).

The eating of **sacramental cakes** at religious festivals was an integral part of the Assyrian and Babylonian worship of "*Ishtar*." The Ancient Egyptians offered small round cakes to "*Hathor*," their cow-headed **moon-goddess**, inscribing the surface of each cake with a pair of curved ox horns. Later, the Greeks replaced the ox-horn symbol with a large cross, representing the four quarters of the moon. These small crossed cakes were also used in the worship of the same goddess as "*Eostre*," the goddess of light and spring. The English title for "*Easter*" is derived from "*Eostre*." So, the custom of eating *"hot cross buns"* became common among Easter celebrations across Europe. The Bible's description of offering cakes and drinks to the *"Queen of Heaven"* eerily mimic the Catholic Mass in general — the **Eucharist**, itself, being a type of rounded wafer cake.

The prophet, Jeremiah, strongly rebuked Israel for worshipping the pagan goddess, but they refused to heed his warning. Consequently, they brought swift destruction upon themselves by the hand of God. Hopefully, the modern *"church"* will be wise enough to recognize the *"Jeremiahs"* of today and heed their warning, but the outlook is not hopeful.

Time magazine reported in an article on December 30, 1991 that *"according to modern Popes"* Mary is *"the* **Queen of the Universe, Queen of Heaven, Seat of Wisdom**. . . ." If Mary is the *"seat of wisdom,"* could the Pope's supposedly infallible words from *"the chair"* really be the words of the veiled Marian goddess? With this order of authority, the Catholic Church looks somewhat different from its public image as a Patriarchal society. Perhaps, the Pope, as *"vicar of Christ,"* is simply Mary's little Christ-child, helping to keep the other children from leaving home (a.k.a. *"the mother church"*).

THE BIBLICAL MARY

What better way for that old serpent, the Devil, to attempt to corrupt the witness of the supernatural **Seed (Jesus Christ)** that would *"crush his head"* than to generate a false supernatural conception (Gen. 3:15). In examining this very detail, however, we find the fatal flaw of his mystical scam — the miraculous component of the false conception supposedly came from *"the woman"* rather than the Lord.

While Queen Semiramis supposedly did not need an outside source of a seed for conception, the Biblical Mary did. The conception in Mary was by the Holy Spirit, by God: "... ***for that which is conceived in her is of the Holy Spirit***" (Mat. 1:20). This was the only way a seed could be truly holy, and it is the reason this supernatural **Seed was called a Savior**! He was the One Whose holiness could save those who identified with Him. Certainly, the Bible emphasizes the virgin-birth for a reason!

It is the devil, on the other hand, who shifts the focus to the virgin-mother. In fact, in the earliest definition of the Babylonian trinity, Queen Semiramis, herself, was said to be the Holy Spirit, the seed of the divine child in the womb. Catholicism teaches the **"Immaculate Conception**," meaning that Mary was born without original sin. Could anything be more blasphemous than claiming another was just as perfect as Christ? Clearly, this **independent woman** did not need God or even a man for that matter. She never could have spent the rest of her days as an ordinary wife and helpmate to Joseph. Queen Semiramis made herself a god and her offspring **little gods**; the Biblical Mary made herself a **humble servant** to be used by the One True God.

And while Mary was certainly a fine and dedicated Godly woman, especially chosen to bear the Body of Jesus, the early church never placed her in an elevated position of spiritual authority; the Disciples never made her divine. In fact, Mary's last recorded words in Scripture pointed away from herself to Jesus Christ. *"His mother saith unto the servants,* **Whatsoever He says unto you, do it**" (Jn. 2:5).

THE BABYLONIAN MOTHER

In Ephesus the Babylonian Mother was *"Diana,"* the Roman virgin goddess of the hunt (which easily connects to Nimrod being a *"mighty hunter"*), the moon, and childbirth. She represented the **creative powers of nature**, so here again we see the time-honored worship of nature headed by the Sun and/or the Moon deity. The temple dedicated to *"Diana"* in Ephesus was actually one of the Seven Wonders of the Ancient World! *"So that not only this our craft is in danger to be set at nought; but also that the Temple of the great goddess Diana should be despised, and her magnificence should be destroyed, whom all Asia and the world worships"* (Acts 19:27).

The Druids worshipped the Mother as the "*Virgo-Paritura*," a virgin about to give birth — in other words, a goddess who was both a **perpetual virgin** and perpetually pregnant. "*Virgo-Paritura*" was understood to forever give birth, "... ***ceaselessly to a world, a god, a humanity in perpetual becoming***" (*Cathedral of the Black Madonna: The Druids and the Mysteries of Chartres*, Jean Markale), so she claimed the ability, not only to independently conceive, but to conceive baby gods as well. She supposedly bore all the numerous pagan gods representing the god-incarnate Nimrod, and although her children are sometimes born mortal, they have only to **realize** their **pre-incarnate divinity** in order to **actualize** their **full potential** as such. This perfectly follows the New Age concept of a universal progressive salvation where an entire **brotherhood** of men strives to reach the fictitious state of "*Christ-consciousness*."

So, we see why the Roman Catholic version of Mary is a perpetual virgin. Her true identity is the Babylonian fertility goddess who remains in her high position of maternal authority among all the pagan religions!

THE FORBIDDEN FRUIT

Certainly, there is something seductive about this religious "*woman*" and the **fruit of her womb** — "*forbidden fruit*" that nourishes a man or woman's alleged "*spark of the divine*" within. It takes us back to the garden when Satan tricked humanity into worshipping him and becoming his slave. Satan became ruler over men by telling them they could be rulers themselves, and by tempting Eve to act as lord of her own life, he was the one who gained the control.

Over time, the counterpart of the pagan "*queen*," (the male-figure, King Nimrod), was essentially pushed out of the picture altogether, only being worshipped in his incarnate form as the child-figure (Tammuz). Therefore, the image of worship and/or picture of the Godhead was complete with just The Mother and The Child.

So, as the pagan religions placed more and more emphasis on

the mother, they did not feel they needed to specifically worship the father-figure at all. In fact, in ancient Babylon, the pagans came to the point of only worshipping the father-figure *"through silence alone."* What a way to remove the name of God! And how much does this sound like today's new spirituality of silent *"meditation,"* *"contemplative prayer,"* or even the esteemed *"moment of silence"* commissioned by our society's leaders in times of hardship and sorrow? Also, text books teach Catholic students prayers of *"inner stillness"* focused on **silent breathing and repetitive, hypnotic speech**, precisely the type of prayer used in New Age spirituality.

In India, the first person (the male-figure) of the Hindu Trinity is no longer worshipped directly, and there are no more temples remaining in his honor. Among the European countries in which Roman Catholicism is the most fully developed, almost all **appearances of the male-figure are missing**. *"The Virgin"* on the other hand, is never hard to find. Every hint of this **blasphemous Godhead** should be destroyed, but it won't be easy, for what could seem more innocent than a mother and her baby?

CATHOLICISM AND CHRISTIANITY

Meanwhile, in complete opposition to the pagan creed, the real Jesus Christ continually emphasized His relationship with the Father, not with Mary. *". . . He who has seen me has seen the Father . . ."* (Jn. 14:9). *"I came forth from the Father, and am come into the world: again, I leave the world, and go to the Father"* (Jn. 16:28). But, because of false doctrine regarding *"the mother,"* many make no attempt to have relationship with the Father.

Catholics regard Mary as the *"**Intercessor**"* and/or *"**Mediator**"* to God, but, in this position, she actually prevents any true worship of the Lord, *"For there is one God, and **one Mediator between God and men, the Man Christ Jesus**"* (I Tim. 2:5).

The deification of *"the mother"* or *"the mother church"* is an intrinsic part of the Babylonian Anti-Christ spirit. The Bible calls this *"woman"* a harlot who commits **spiritual adultery** with the "*kings of the earth*" and leads the church away from her true **Husband, Jesus Christ** (Rev. 17:2).

High priestesses of the occult world readily agree that Christianity is the only religion that, in fact, does not recognize some form of a principal female deity. And accordingly, Catholic versions of Genesis 3:15 have often been translated that, "... ***she (the woman) would bruise thy head* . . .**" rather than the true Biblical translation that ". . . ***it (the seed; Christ) shall bruise thy head. . . .***"

Undeniably, Catholicism and true Christianity are not the same faith! Genuine Believers have always had to defend the True Christian Faith against the counterfeit religion of Catholicism.

CHAPTER ELEVEN

THE TRINITY

The Bible clearly defines the **Trinity** as God the Father, God the Son, and God the Holy Spirit — One God manifested in Three Persons who are in complete union. While the Three Members of the Trinity may perform separate functions, the Trinity cannot be separated. There is One God. If you truly find One Member, you have, at the same time, found the Others as well, and One never works disconnectedly from the Others.

Certainly, the concept of the Trinity is difficult for the human mind to understand, so it makes perfect sense that pagans would prefer to imitate something from this earthly life that they can identify with — like the human family. And sure enough, just as the Catholics have adopted other pagan traditions, they have adopted the pagan family Trinity as well. According to the Chronology of Biblical History by R.C. Wetzel, the Council of Nicea established the Trinity as *"God the Father, the Virgin Mary, and Messiah their Son."* If Mary is considered part of the Trinity, Mary is automatically considered to be God. As we have already stated, none of the Apostles or the Lord Jesus Christ even hinted at the idea of **Mary-worship**; the *Encyclopedia Britannica* confirms that during the first centuries of the church, no emphasis was placed upon Mary whatsoever. It was not until the time of Constantine (the early part of the Fourth Century) that anyone even thought about considering Mary divine (Vol. 14 p.309). Epiphanies even denounced certain women of Thrace, Arabia, and elsewhere, for worshipping her as a goddess and offering cakes at her shrine. Yet to this day, Mary-worship has not only been condoned by the Catholic Church, it has become one of her most predominantly practiced doctrines.

MARY WORSHIP

Often, when one tries to tell a Catholic follower that he worships Mary, he responds with emphatic declarations of *"**honor**"* rather than *"**worship**."* But once you agree to honor something, there is always the danger to begin to make an idol of it; it is a fine line to walk in any situation. And unfortunately, just a short review of some of Catholicism's most **sacred prayers** shows us that the Catholic's veneration of Mary crossed that line a long time ago. *"**The Rosary**"* requires one to recite the *"**Hail Mary**"* prayer numerous times, and *"**The Rosary**"* always ends with the prayer, *"**Hail, Holy Queen**."*

*"**Hail Mary**"* is recited as follows: *"**Hail Mary, full of grace, the Lord is with you; blessed are you among women, and blessed is the fruit of your womb, Jesus. Holy Mary, Mother of God, pray for us sinners now and at the hour of our death. Amen.**"*

Here are the words of *"**Hail, Holy Queen**"*: *"**Hail, Holy Queen, Mother of Mercy; hail, our life, our sweetness, and our hope! To you do we cry, poor banished children of Eve; to you do we send up our sighs, mourning, and weeping in this vale of tears. Turn, then, most gracious advocate, your eyes of mercy toward us; and after this our exile, show unto us the blessed fruit of your womb, Jesus, O clement, O loving, O sweet Virgin Mary!**"*

*"**The Angelus**"* prayer includes these words: *"**. . . Pray for us, O Holy Mother of God, that we may be worthy of the promises of Christ. . . .**"*

In the *"**Memorare**"* prayer, one must say, *"**Remember, O most gracious Virgin Mary, that never was it known that anyone who fled to your protection, implored your help, or sought your intercession was left unaided. Inspired with this confidence, we fly unto you, O Virgin of virgins, our Mother. To you we come, before you we kneel, sinful and sorrowful. . . .**"*

POPE JOHN PAUL II

The late Pope John Paul II further demonstrates Catholicism's improper deification of Mary when he wrote this concerning her: **"On the universal level, if victory comes it will be brought by Mary, Christ will conquer through her because he wants the church's victories now and in the future to be linked to her"** (*"Crossing the Threshold of Hope,"* 1994; *Our Lady Publication.* Spring, 1995). John Paul II was so convinced that Mary intervened to save him during the attempt on his life, he left the bullet that was removed from his body in the golden crown of the *"Madonna"* during his visit in 1991. John Paul II **"has dedicated himself and a Pontificate to our Lady."** He did bear the letter *"M"* in his Coat of Arms for Mary, and his personal motto (embroidered on the side of his robes) was the following: *"**Totus Tuus Sum Maria**."* In English, this Latin phrase translates to, *"**Mary, I'm all Yours**."*

True Christians, on the other hand, belong to Jesus Christ alone; He is the One who bought and paid for them with His own precious Blood at Calvary. *". . . you are not your own? For you are bought with a price: therefore Glorify God in your body, and in your spirit, which are God's"* (I Cor. 6:19-20).

Pope John Paul's *"M"* resembled the astrological symbol for Virgo as well, which attached a looped *"v"* to an *"M."* Astrologers practicing this form of divination associated Virgo with the Virgin Mary in medieval times. She was, therefore, symbolized with an *"M"* or *"MV"* (*"Maria Virgo"* or *"Virgin Mary"*). She was often pictured in her role as a goddess of agricultural fertility with sheaves of wheat or corn in her hand; in other words, it was understood that she insured the **fruitfulness of all the earth** as well.

MOTHER OF GOD?

Another deceptive and indoctrinating title for Mary is *"**mother of god**."* This phrase actually leaves the offensive impression that Mary existed before God, making her a preexistent deity.

But, nothing gave birth to God. He was not created in any way. **He is the Creator, the Alpha and the Omega, the First and the Last, the Beginning and the End!** Author Dave Hunt explains that Mary was the mother of Jesus, but in his humanity, not in his deity, *"She was not his mother as God . . . She is the mother of the physical body which the Son of God took when He became man . . ."* (*A Woman Rides the Beast* p.438).

But Pope John Paul II continues to indulge in the idolatrous worship of his lady god as he calls Mary, "*. . .* **Mother of the Church, Queen of the Apostles . . . [and] dwelling place of the Trinity!**" Again, while Christ was once birthed from Mary's womb, one could in no way claim that Mary houses the Trinity. In Egypt, however, the mother goddess was called *"Athor,"* the "**Habitation of God**," signifying that the *"fullness of the godhead"* dwelt in her womb. This title, the *"habitation of god,"* also corresponds with the New Age idea of *"***Mother Earth***"* — *"Mother Earth"* being the habitation that maintains all humanity, and some today falsely believe that this human race will actually **incarnate Christ** as it reaches its full spiritual maturity, creating a *"***new breed***"* of supermen on the earth. How many times must we remind people that they cannot become God?

EL SHADDAI

But, Who supplies the earth? — the Lord. He alone is the Source. Christians do not have to **trust nature**; we trust in God! And furthermore, the Bible has clearly shown us that **this world is not our home**. The Lord has prepared a **home for us in Heaven** where we will dwell with Him forever. In fact, when you are saved, you are already spiritually placed in Heavenly Places with Christ. *"And has raised us up together, and made us sit together in* **Heavenly Places** *in Christ Jesus"* (Eph. 2:6). "***LORD, You have been our dwelling place in all generations****. Before the mountains were brought forth, or ever You had formed the Earth and the world, even from everlasting to everlasting, You are God"* (Ps. 90:1-2). *"But I have built a* **House of habitation** *for You, and a place for Your dwelling for ever"* (II Chron. 6:2).

The *"mother goddess"* of Babylon even had the nerve to claim that she nourished the people, providing all nutritional and spiritual needs to those from her womb. But again, Scripture clearly points to Another, One outside this fallen world.

The Lord is called "***El Shaddai***," indicating that all nourishment comes from Him alone. Just as a baby is completely sustained by his mother's milk, Believers are likewise, totally nourished by the Lord (the term "*El Shaddai*" refers to "*the breast*"). The earth has no life-giving power, and it is not a **sacred entity** that creates physical and/or spiritual food independent of God's Hand. It is the Lord who causes the plants to grow, rain to fall, and babies to be born, and likewise, it is the Lord who feeds the hungry soul. **He is our Provider, our All in All!** So, while the pagans and their Catholic friends claim to receive sustenance from the Earth, the creation, or "*mother*" nature, Christians claim and proclaim, El Shaddai! — the Creator who provides for all our needs! "*But my God shall **supply all your need** according to His riches in Glory by Christ Jesus*" (Phil. 4:19).

THE CHURCH?

Yes, the pagans were well-acquainted with their "*mother*" before the True New Testament Church of the Lord Jesus Christ was ever formed. But what a glorious Church it was in those early days! Its convicting Truth of Jesus Christ could not be silenced, and though it may have been small in number, it was measureless in the steadfast strength of the Lord. The evil "*mother and god-child*" was no match for the True Gospel of a Loving Savior.

In view of this fact, it is heartbreaking to see that by the Third and Fourth Centuries, the "*church*" was blown by **ecumenical winds of change** and began falling into the **apostasy** the apostles had warned about. The "*church*" had greatly departed from its **fundamental faith**, its **new theology** being built upon the most common elements of diverse religions. **Unity became the new gospel as all other values and truths fell at its feet.** Now all seekers were pleased to venture into the church, and little by little, paganism began to flourish right within the professing Catholic "*church*" of Rome! (II Tim. 4:3).

Sounds exactly like the modern church-growth concept, doesn't it? You can just hear many of today's *"pastors"* telling people that they do not have to give up their religiously – inclined practices like psychiatry to exhibit Faith in Christ. *"No man can serve **two masters**: for either he will hate the one, and love the other; or else he will hold to the one, and despise the other. You cannot serve God and mammon"* (Mat. 6:24).

THE GOSPEL

In fact, many mistakenly think these idols are simply just **Christ** *"outside the box"*, when, in reality, these misguided people are the ones trying to stuff Jesus in a box — a box He doesn't fit in! And Jesus won't change His **shape** to fit in that box either; He doesn't accommodate the Devil or fallen man.

On the other hand, it is man's flawed personality that God will alter. By the grace of God, what you are is not what you are going to be! This is the Gospel — to be changed by the Power of God! Nothing man is born with is of any use to God; it is only what man has allowed God to mold within him (through yielding to the Holy Spirit) that makes him a vessel God can use.

This is why it is a gigantic waste of time for false shepherds to be encouraging members of his flock to discover attributes of *"self"* or personal *"shape"* (Purpose Driven Life, ch. 29-35, Rick Warren). If God has anything to do with it, *"self"* will be changed, Hallelujah!

And so certainly that *"**pagan-permissive**"* **"church"** of **Rome**, with its masses of unchanged people and practices, could well be the original model of today's *"**seeker-sensitive**"* **"church"** of **America**, and it is a horrific tragedy that both have swiftly taken the apostate church back home to its Babylonian *"mother."* ***"And upon her forehead was a name written, MYSTERY, BABYLON THE GREAT, THE MOTHER OF HARLOTS AND ABOMINATIONS OF THE EARTH"*** (Rev. 17:5).

PAGAN INFLUENCES

And since the Catholic Church has so openly allowed pagan

influences to infiltrate the church, it has been overtaken with **delusion**. The gross **superstitions** that have accompanied the use of **relics** very clearly reveal the tragic deception and inconsistency with which Romanism has been plagued for centuries. Most of these relics are so obviously fake, it is extremely hard to comprehend that people in this century of advanced knowledge could believe they have any type of significance whatsoever. But unfortunately, the ultimate consequence of compromise is that you lose all sight of the truth.

Relics, in general, are remains from a time passed; they may also represent an object, culture, or person in particular from that time. The problem comes when these relics mix with various forms of spirituality and become **religious charms** and/or **amulets** that are falsely believed to either possess the Power of God and/or bring the Presence of God to a specific location. It is thought that since a relic has been part of a god or near to a god at some time in the past it has somehow preserved the power of that god as well. However, the truth is that it is only Faith — Faith in the Finished Work of the Cross — that can receive the Power of God.

And sadly, this same concept involving the **fabricated powers of inanimate objects** is prominent among people controlled by a **spirit of gambling**. If you have ever visited a gambling casino, many of its regulars never arrive without their rabbit's foot, 4-leaf clover, horseshoe, or other item they believe in. The only real difference is that the secular gambler's gods, who are believed to respond to such objects, have names like *"luck," "fortune,"* and *"fate."* Most often the only explanation for the addict's belief in a particular charm is the object's connection with *"luck"* at some point in the past.

RELICS

Some of the most common relics of the Catholic Church have been pieces of the supposed *"true cross"* of Christ. Besides the fact that there is obviously no spiritual power in a piece of wood, it doesn't take a genius to see that all these pieces could not have been a part of the original Cross, for there were certainly more than enough to make a single wooden beam. As a matter of fact, there were enough pieces scattered throughout Europe to make a forest!

Other notable relics that have received Papal approval through the centuries include nails from the Cross, the sponge lifted to Christ's mouth, the purple coat which was thrown over Christ's shoulders by the mocking soldiers, the crown of thorns, the cup of the Last Supper, specimens of the Virgin Mary's hair (some blond, some brown, some red, and some black), skirts of the Virgin, Mary's wedding ring, Mary's slippers, the swaddling clothes of the baby Jesus, Joseph's carpentry tools, one of the "*thirty pieces of silver*," the empty purse of Judas, Pilate's basin, and even the bones of the ass upon which Jesus made his entry into Jerusalem.

Amazingly, the stupidity of this profane and idolatrous fiasco only continues to get worse. Though we know nothing of the Mother of Mary (not even her name as Catholic scholars admit), the Catholic Church decided to just give her the name St. Anne a few hundred years ago. A couple of churches in Europe actually claimed to keep her body as a sacred relic. One body is supposed to be in Apte, France, another in Lyons, and besides these bodies, relics of her head were supposedly at Trier, at Luren, and still another at Luringe.

Several renowned relics were housed at the "*Tabernacle of Mary Magdalene*" as well. This Tabernacle claimed to have the towel Jesus used to wipe the Disciple's feet, the napkin that covered Jesus' Face in the tomb, Mary's veil, some of Mary's clothes, and even a bottle of the Virgin's milk! And even more absurdly, some of Mary's milk is supposed to have colored the walls of the place called the "*Milk Grotto*" at Bethlehem, and pieces of this chalk-rock are sold as relic charms.

The use of relics can indeed be found throughout all false religious systems of the past and the present. Even the infamous hero-worship of the Greeks included great regard for the bones of their deified warriors. In fact, among several religions, the very foundations for relic-obsession come from legends of striking similarity. Like Nimrod, the bones and/or limbs of Osiris were said to have been scattered across the land after his death, and the same applies to the legend of the death of Buddha. The first duty of his descendents and followers were **collect these bones and entomb them**. The Babylonian Zoroaster (a.k.a. Nimrod) was also said to have "... *charged his countrymen to preserve his remains* ..." (Hislop, *The Two Babylons*, p.180). Since these bones were considered sacred, the very ground or tomb in which one of them was buried was considered to be sacred as well. This became the justification for the many **pilgrimages** made to such grounds and the many requests for personal burial at these sites.

Quite interestingly, the meeting place of the Skull and Bones, an elite Yale fraternity, is referred to as The Tomb and houses many mysterious relics. The members, called Bonesmen, have included many of the Twentieth Century's most powerful people including our current president. It is said that, Prescott Bush, George W. Bush's grandfather, and a band of fellow Bonesmen robbed the grave of Geronimo, taking the skull of this Apache Indian chief back with them to their Tomb.

CHAPTER TWELVE

THE SALE OF BONES

In around the time of 750, long lines of wagons could be seen coming to Rome in a constant stream, bringing immense quantities of **skulls and skeletal bones**, which would be **sorted, labeled, and sold by the Popes. Almost immediately, the sale of these skulls and bones became big business!** (*Medieval Italy* p.71). There is a marble slab in the Church of St. Prassede, which states that in 817 Pope Paschal had the **bodies of 2,300 martyrs transferred from cemeteries to the church**! And, why not? Certainly the more products you have, the more of them you can sell, and indeed every **pilgrim to Rome** was anxious to acquire such relics since they desperately desired the use of their alleged powers.

People began to do whatever it took to get them. Graves were plundered and robbed by night, and churches even had to be watched by armed men. *"Rome"* says Gregoroviues *"was like a smouldering cemetery in which hyenas howled and fought as they dug greedily after corpses."*

Let's face it; man needs power, a power greater than themselves — not only for Salvation, but to deal with the sure hardships of every day life. **Humanity needs the Power of God**, but somehow, *"church"* fathers had become spiritual crypt-keepers guarding lifeless bones rather than ministers sharing the True Power of God, the Power which can only be found in the Message of the Cross of Jesus Christ. *"For the preaching of the Cross is to them who perish foolishness; but unto us which are saved it is the Power of God"* (I Cor. 1:18). See, **when you distribute the Gospel, you distribute the Power of God!** Jesus said, *"Woe unto you, Scribes and Pharisees, hypocrites! for you are like unto whited sepulchres,* *which indeed appear beautiful outward, but are within full of dead men's bones, and of all uncleanness"* (Mat. 23:27).

UNGODLY SUPERSTITION

The church in Coulombs, France was just one of the many major promoters of false relic power. It claimed to possess what was known as the *"Holy Prepuce"* (the prepuce is the tiny portion of skin that is removed from a baby boy when he is circumcised). Just how this Catholic Church in France came into the possession of the supposed prepuce of Jesus so many years later is, of course, a mystery, just like everything else in *"mystery Babylon"* (Rev. 17:5). (Actually, circumcision in Jesus' time only removed the tip of the foreskin. And secondly, Jewish custom was that it was immediately buried in the ground. It was Charlemagne who initially claimed he received it as a gift from **the Angel Gabriel**.)

Its powers were highly acclaimed during this time period. It was believed to contain the power to make childless women fertile and the process of childbirth completely safe. Henry V of England so faithfully accepted its **doctrine of false power** that when Queen Catherine was to have her child (heir to the British throne), he made arrangements to borrow the prepuce just for the occasion. Sounds a little like many in the modern day church who think they can borrow someone else's *"anointing,"* doesn't it? As it turns out, Henry's wife had no complications in childbirth, and so, the idiotic **superstition was further solidified by this misguiding *"sign."*** Because of the event, Henry even built a sanctuary at Columbus for the prepuce's safe-keeping, and of course, as its story spread, it was not long until other churches also claimed to possess the *"Holy Prepuce,"* including the Church of St. John in Rome and the Church of Puy in Velay (*The Other Side of Rome* p. 54). This also reminds me of some of our modern day preachers that sell what they purport to be *"holy oil."*

Many of the *"sacred relics"* have been proven, beyond question, to be fake anyway. For example, some of the acclaimed bones of the saints and martyrs have been exposed to be the bones of animals. One

Cathedral in Spain displayed what was said to be part of Gabriel's wing, but upon further investigation, it was found that this supposed angel wing was really an ostrich feather (*Roman Catholicism* p. 290).

In light of such ridiculous inconsistency, what else might possibly be influencing Catholics to ascribe so much importance to relics? Well, another major part of the problem is that the placement of a relic in a chapel or cathedral is believed to "*consecrate*" or somehow sanctify that specific building or ground (*Medieval Italy* p. 71). Of course, it is utter stupidity to think that a relic or anything else can make a soulless piece of land "*holy*," but, regardless, it is that strong belief in the relic that prevails.

This belief became so extreme during the Middle Ages that Cathedrals often had thousands of relics. The Castle Church at Wittenberg, upon whose door Luther nailed his famous "*95 Theses*", possessed 19,000 saintly relics (*Durant* Vol. 6 p.339). In 787, the Seventh Ecumenical Council of Nicea forbade a bishop to dedicate a building if no relics were present; the penalty for doing such was excommunication from the church!

Similarly, we see a phenomenon called **spiritual-mapping** in the modern church where Christians believe that their targeted prayers have warred against demonic strongholds in a specified city and won. Now, that city has been "*set apart*" or "*consecrated*" for the Lord. In this case, it is a strong belief in their prayers rather than a relic, but both are wrong because they sidestep belief in Calvary's Cross. While it is certainly Biblical and expedient for the Child of God to pray, prayer itself — whether memorized prayers, silent prayers, walking prayers, loud prayers, stationed (labyrinth-style) prayers, or repetitive prayers — is not the power source no matter how you dress it up.

RELIC WORSHIP

Since the pagan religion is steeped in relic-worship, we can easily see that the Catholic Church, again, borrowed from pagan Babylon to inherit its neurotic beliefs about relic power, not to mention that there is no Biblical indication of this belief by the Lord Jesus or any of the Apostles. Remember the death of Nimrod (false *"savior"* of Babylon). Notice that there is a striking contrast between his death and the death of the True Savior, Jesus Christ. Nimrod was torn limb from limb; concerning Jesus, it was prophesied that, *"a bone of Him shall not be broken."* When Nimrod was supposedly resurrected to become the sun-god, it was taught that he left the members of his old body behind. However, such could not be termed a ***"resurrection"*** in the true sense of the word like in the case with Christ. Jesus was truly resurrected! Remember, the **tomb was empty**! Empty! It was His entire Being that rose from the dead! Even if someone had wanted to, no part of Christ's Body was available to be used for relics. **Our Savior rose again and is alive forevermore!**

Continuing to follow the legends of Nimrod's death, parts of his remaining body were scattered and buried in separate places. Then, as time went on, more fabrications developed as to specifically where the locations of these burial sites were. Again, since the relic was considered sacred, it had made these burial sites *"sacred"* too, and naturally, the same notions where found in other nations of pagan worship regarding their false martyred god. Various places in Egypt, for example, took on special spiritual significance. *"Egypt was covered with sepulchers of its martyred god; and many a leg and arm and skull, all vouched to be genuine, were exhibited in the rival burying-places for the adoration of the Egyptian faithful"* (*The Two Babylons* p. 179).

Pilgrimages, thereby, became a major part of participating in all pagan religion to obtain greater spiritual sanction, knowledge, or power. These journeys are also prominent among Muslims. They travel to Mecca, the holy city of Islam.

PILGRIMAGES?

Christians, however, do not make any pilgrimages to any tombs to worship any bones; there is no basis in Scripture whatsoever for making such pilgrimages to the tombs of Saints, Martyrs, Prophets, or Apostles. In fact, the very way in which the Lord saw fit to dispose of the body of Moses indicates our Lord's opposition to the idea of pilgrimages made to adore religious idols. We know Moses was buried in the plains of Moab, but the exact spot is unknown (Deut. 34:6). God's wisdom in keeping this information a secret is certainly obvious; He knows how readily the human heart worships idols.

Remember that the Israelites set up of the golden calf, and years after that, even worshipped the brass serpent that Moses had made and named *"Nehushtan"* (II Ki.18:4). How sad when a *"church"* trades the Presence of God, for the presence of insensible structures built by the hand or mind of man. *"For My people have committed two evils; they have forsaken Me the fountain of living waters, and hewed them out cisterns, broken cisterns, that can hold no water"* (Jer. 2:13).

Even during the Middle Ages, one of the most popular ways of *"washing away sin"* was to make a pilgrimage to the Holy Sepulcher in Jerusalem.

Still today, there are new heretical books being written as a result of such **sacred journeys** and the artifacts found there. Listen to the words of this modern day *"Christian"* author, Michael Baigent, who wrote the newly released *The Jesus Papers* as he comments on his inspiration: *"I love to travel to sacred sites and to feel them, to seek to understand them. . . . Are such places intrinsically sacred, or do we make them so? Perhaps both. Sacred sites demand participation from the visitor, an entering into a relationship with them, an experience. And there lies the difference between a pilgrim and a tourist."*

Then, upon viewing what he claims were letters written by Jesus to the Sanhedrin, Baigent creates the perilous illusion that there may be extra-biblical knowledge of Jesus, which the church should seek to find. Just the opposite is true; the church should be seeking to understand what we already know is the revealed Truth, the Word of God.

WORLDLY GAIN!

So, while the Catholic Church is giving its followers all kinds of mystical means to power, it has been using some very different and very practical tactics to secure its own livelihood. In fact, the methods the Catholic Church have employed have a whole lot more to do with the worldly gain of its institution than the spiritual gain of its followers.

What is the best way to insure power in the world? Well, of course, to have the most money. The entire system of man and his ways of success, influence, and authority largely depend on this one thing, so if you want worldly power, you must have the financial backing!

Of course, Jesus was not interested in collecting assets. He said: "***Lay not up for yourselves treasures upon earth***, *where moth and rust does corrupt, and where thieves break through and steal*" (Mat. 6:19).

As we will see, however, the Catholic "*church*," has the largest treasure-trove of any entity on Earth today, including its overflowing bank accounts, real estate, stock investments, priceless artistic works, etc. The wealth of the Catholic Church is, in fact, so vast that there is no way to officially calculate the total. It exists in many, many forms of which only some are openly displayed to the public. Others take painstaking research to dig out, so there is essentially no way to track it all, but to be sure, there is not a single area of financial endeavor that the Catholic Church has not tapped into.

One of Murphy's laws says that, *"whoever has the gold makes the rules."* So, does the Catholic Church want to control the world? The answer is, *"yes,"* and according to this golden rule, she already does!

The Vatican's treasury of solid gold, largely stored in gold ingots with the U.S. Federal Reserve Bank, while banks in England and Switzerland hold the rest, has been estimated by the "*United Nations World Magazine*" to amount to several billion dollars. In the Seventies and Eighties, the financial reserves of the Vatican equaled those of both France and Britain. The United Kingdom's dollar reserves were estimated at $1,000 million, but this was only the equivalent to one-fifth of the Vatican's marketable stock, which were between 5,000 and 6,000 million dollars. The Vatican, at this same time, had a gold reserve of $11 billion, which was three times the gold reserve of all of Great Britain! By the Eighties, the volume of the Vatican's world-wide stocks and shares was 5 to 10 billion dollars. The Vatican's wealth in just the Italian peninsula, including stocks, shares, real estate, and direct and indirect involvement in industrial and commercial enterprise, has been described by the British periodical, *"The Economist"*, in this way, *"it could theoretically throw the Italian economy into confusion if it decided to unload all its shares suddenly and dump them on the market"* (Manhattan, Avro. *The Vatican Billions*, p. 200). Undoubtedly, the Vatican is the world's largest shareholder, and these sums, remember, are only the Vatican's *"liquid capital reserves."* The monstrosity of its wealth only begins here.

Besides its business assets, it has other sources of wealth which, although they are intangible and invisible, are just as real and valuable. For instance, the Catholic Church is the largest owner of **historic**, **architectural**, **and artistic buildings** in the world, such as the Florence Cathedral or St. Peter's Basilica, and the very lands upon which many of them are built are worth incalculable amounts as they are located in renowned ancient cities. In an open market, the Sistine Chapel alone would be worth between 250 and 500 million dollars.

The buildings also contain many valuable ecclesiastical and sacred objects as well; these buildings and objects have another material value called *"historicity,"* which means that they have acquired a considerable amount of **antique value**, in addition to their intrinsic worth. For instance, a gold chalice, in addition to its actual gold, could actually be worth a thousand times more because of its historicity. Also, the statues and sculptures that fill most Catholic churches are covered in **gold**, **silver**, **precious stones**, **rare pearls**,

diamonds, etc. At the lowest estimate, these costly valuables would collect hundreds of millions of dollars at any contemporary antique auction. The Catholic Church is also the greatest lover of art throughout all time; her **art collection alone makes her a multi-billionaire**, and these artistic works will continue to increase in value every year! (Manhattan, p. 281-283). The Vatican also owns many ancient manuscripts which, if sold, would bring in another immeasurable millions of dollars.

All of this also excludes the many and varied ways the Catholic Church has abused its spiritual authority to rob from its poor followers such as the sale of indulgences, payments for mass, church tax, etc. which will be discussed in more detail later.

MORE AND MORE WEALTH

By no means is the wealth of the Catholic Church limited to the Vatican or other foreign countries; she is also the richest conglomerate in America as well. *"It was done by the urge to proselytize. By the urge to become respectable, powerful, and superior. By the belief that, being the only true church, it is her mission, duty, and obligation to convert the U.S. into a fief of Eternal Rome"* (Manhattan, Avro. *The Vatican Billions*, 157).

One of the most powerful orders of the Roman Catholic church, the Jesuits, originally furnished A.P.Giannini with half of the starting capital for the Bank of America, and today they own at least 51% of its stock. They are also one of the largest stockbrokers in the American steel company, Republic and National, and among the most important owners of the four greatest aircraft manufacturing companies in the U.S., Boeing, Lockheed, Douglas, and Curtis-Wright. They also have dominating interest in Phillips Oil Company and Creole Petroleum Co.

Though the Jesuits may perhaps be the wealthiest, there are hundreds and hundreds of such Catholic orders, both male and female, infiltrating the U.S. They are just as numerous as the ones throughout Europe.

The Jesuit order alone brings in an income of at least between $250; and $280 million a year, and being a religious organization, also has **tax exemption status** in the U.S. — just as all Catholic religious orders do! The combined assets of Catholic religious orders have been estimated to be at least $24 billion. If we add to this the mass of property, investments, industrial shares, etc. owned by the Catholic Church, by 1968, the wealth of Catholicism's purely religious functioning in America was estimated to be greater than, $54 billion.

Of course, this is only the openly expressed financial assets of the Catholic "*church*" in America. There is much more under the guise of her commercial operations. Just to mention one example, a Washington, D.C. luxury housing project valued at $75 million was announced by Societa General Immobilaire of Rome, which is a subsidiary of the Vatican. The Vatican also has shares worth $100 million between the companies of American Anaconda Copper and Sinclair Oil, and it has been a major player in the purchase and sale of gold in the U.S. Also, the amount of government money from federal tax dollars given to aid Catholic organizations (many of which are in the educational and medical field) is staggering. One telling figure reports that in 1966, $30.5 million of taxpayers' money was given to them.

Among some more of the companies into which the Catholic Church has placed hundreds of stock and bond investments is Baltimore and Ohio R.R., Missouri Pacific, Goodyear, Firestone, Commonwealth Edison, Brooklyn Edison, N.Y. Edison, Pacific Gas and Electric, Texas Electric, Atlantic City Convention Hall, Fox Theater, Thermoid, and Pillsbury Flour. Of course, the list goes on and on.

Larson and Lowell investigators once estimated the Catholic wealth in the U.S., including such items as annual voluntary income, stocks, bonds, real estate, commercial business property, and religiously used real estate; the estimate came to at least $80 billion. One can only imagine what it would be today. "*By 1972,* *the combined assets of the U.S.'s five largest industrial corporations totaled about $46.9 billion . . . the virtue of this, the Catholic Church, therefore, has become the mightiest corporation of the U.S.,* **a colossus before which the wealth of even the most powerful American concerns shrink into insignificance**. *Thus, within a single generation, she has contrived to transform herself into the* **wealthiest giant theocracy of the western hemisphere, if not the entire world**' (Manhattan, p. 188).

# CHAPTER THIRTEEN

BELIEVING

Any type of **erroneous belief** is the real problem, whether belief in a physical object, a person, or an abstract concept. Belief contains a controlling power in and of itself, because what a person believes very effectively determines what he does. Belief has a dangerous side effect as well. Once the mind has accepted something as truth, anything desirable that may occur afterward is often considered to be a *"sign"* or *"confirmation"* of that belief, or you might say one has *"experienced"* that belief. Even if the favorable outcome is purely **coincidental**, people tend to attribute it to their own belief system simply to further their justification of *"self."* As we have seen, Catholics often attribute blessings to their use of relics simply because they have already believed the lie of relic-power. Man operates in some sort of believing faith far more than he realizes; he is not as rational as he thinks!

This is why correct believing must come before *"**signs**"* and *"**wonders**."* Even if the *"sign"* or *"wonder"* is inherently **miraculous**, the belief must be right, totally and completely separate from what may look like *"confirmation."* Otherwise, the miracles a person ends up following may not be from God.

Some preachers have even marketed pieces of their shirt, drenched in their perspiration, claiming it had miraculous power. I remember seeing Juanita Bynum on TBN rolling over and over on sheets and sending little pieces of the sheets to people who would call in with an offering. Juanita claimed that ordinary pieces of cloth were anointed with the power of God just because they had touched the presence of God that had been supposedly flowing through her service that day.

But, **spiritually soaking** an object (or a person) does not somehow transfer a deposit of God's Power to it. The Source is forever the *"Lamb that was slain,"* Jesus Christ, Who is only accessible by Faith! While it is true that the Power of God may flow through a person at times, the Power is never coming from the person. It is being supplied through Faith in Christ.

SCAM ARTISTS

The *"church,"* however, is filled with people who teach otherwise; they pose as preachers and twist the Word of God to trick people into thinking that giving money will make them wealthy! For instance, you might hear them promise that if you donate a specific amount of money, you will be debt-free by the end of the year.

Just recently, there have been *"preachers"* on the INSP television network soliciting money by creating a false belief regarding the Jewish holiday, **Passover**. They twist Exodus, Chapter 23, claiming that if you give them a Passover offering, God has seven special blessings He will give you in return. They forget to mention, however, that Christians no longer need to bring a Passover offering because Jesus Christ, the Lamb of God, was that Offering! He has already paid for all your blessings, including the most precious blessing of all — the Salvation of your soul.

Yes, God does bless His children, but we must always remember that the **blessing of God cannot be obtained by money or other works of the flesh**. Works of the flesh are always the result of faulty beliefs (or law).

Schemes of this nature have actually been around for a long time; they are nothing new, and in the long-run they only end-up benefiting the preachers (or popes). Clerics line their pockets, but their parishioners are left high and dry. Tragically, when the *"blessings"* do not come, the laity are told that they simply do not have enough faith. But, it wasn't that they didn't have the faith; it was that their **faith was in all the wrong objects**! The Finished Work of the Cross is the only Object in which Faith should ever be placed.

THE CHURCH AND THE STATE

World domination has, in fact, been Rome's intentional **goal**, her *"**vision**,"* for many centuries; she has claimed ownership of all lands of the earth, all in the name of God. Her *"**Promised land**"* is essentially, the world.

Beginning with the Donation of Constantine in A.D. 315, we see a progression of papal decrees and other manipulations of church power to reinforce its ideals, building a foundational belief within the Roman Catholic system that she should, indeed, inherit all the Earth. Once Catholics believed in this **purpose of the church**, as decreed by the heralded **prophets of God** (the popes), they became **voluntary soldiers in the pope's army**.

Amazingly, the **great vision of Roman dominionism** became reality; the unexpected part was that instead of the popes being subject to the emperors, the emperors became subject to the *"infallible"* vicars of Christ. You see, it takes a religious/spiritual element to successfully keep people's **allegiance**, and to help boost this **loyalty**, the people were taught that speaking against the pope's decrees meant speaking against God. Unfortunately, they had been **taught to equate *"church government"* with the Lord**.

Any true servant of God who would speak out against these false prophets would be labeled *"***divisive***"* or of having a *"***rebellious spirit**,*"* and then they could only await the impending punishment that would come with such a despised stand. And just as Christ was put on the Cross for His stand against false religious government, many of these were martyred for their stand as well. Jesus said, *"But take heed to yourselves: for they shall deliver you up to councils; and in the Synagogues you shall be beaten: and you shall be brought before rulers and kings for my sake, for a testimony against them"* (Mk. 13:9).

According to the Donation, Constantine had given the Pope and his successors, as vicars of Christ on earth, authority over large

128 The Modern Babylon

territories of land extending outside of Rome, as well as the Lateran Palace and Rome itself. It was essentially all of Constantine's Empire including all of France, Spain, Britain, and the rest of the entirety of Europe, which made the Roman Empire a fief of the papacy.

CATHOLIC CLAIMS

Pope Innocent IV went even further to say that what Constantine had given the pope was not really his to give in the first place, that, in actuality, the *"church"* had always owned Europe; Innocent said that the Donation was "*. . . but a visible sign of his* **sovereign dominion over the whole world, and hence of all the wealth to be found on earth**" (Manhattan, Avro, *The Vatican Billions*, p. 42).

The *"vicars of Christ"* also claimed authority over all kings as well, "*. . . every monarch, even the most powerful, possesses only so much power and territory as the pope has transferred to him or finds good to allow him . . . it was Christ who had entrusted Peter and his successors both powers, the sacerdotal and the royal, the* **reign of both kingdoms, the heavenly and the earthly**, *belonged to him, the pope: by which he meant that the spiritual dominion of the papacy had to have its counterpart also in* **papal dominion over all the lands, territories, and riches of the entire world**" (p.44).

Emperors and kings swore to defend the *"church"* by the sword. Later papal decrees would specifically claim ownership of all lands yet to be discovered, including the Americas.

Now, considering the magnitude of the effects that began with this heralded Donation, can you believe that the document, itself, was not even legitimate? By analyzing the Donation's language and showing that some of the Latin used in it could not have been written in the Fourth Century. Lorenzo Valla, a papal aid, proved that the document was a forgery in 1440, and this is still recognized by historians today. Also, the date given in the Donation does not correspond to several other historical evidences indicating the time of its writing.

THE FRANK LIE

So, in reality, the popes of Rome stole their so-called Papal States from the rightful owners of the land. They mercilessly controlled, taxed, and derived great wealth from these lands.

And not only has the Catholic Church made the unbiblical claim that it has the right, given by the authority of God's representatives on earth, to make slaves of people in foreign lands, its claim is based on the **frank lie**. If this isn't taking the name of the Lord in vain, I don't know what is!

Actually, the Catholic Church did not officially gain their papal lands until A.D. 756, when the *"Donation of Pepin"* gave the legal right for Papal States, extending papal rule beyond the traditional diocese of Rome. Interestingly, this turned out to be one of the most effective cases in which the Donation of Constantine aided the Catholic Church in its quest for worldly authority.

In fact, it may have been its original purpose since Pepin's gift occurred around the approximate time of the Donation's first known appearance. When Pepin, the new King of France, was presented with the Donation, he immediately granted Pope Stephen II and the Church its papal lands; this way Pepin could conveniently claim he was returning, rather than giving, the pope the lands, and as an added bonus for Pepin, he would receive the favor of the *"church,"* and thus, with God.

Such circumstances of **fraud, deceit, and selfish ambition** are not unusual though; as we have seen, the Roman Catholic Church has functioned in this manner during its entire existence. Many **forged documents** were used to further their dominion. Even after Valla published his work thoroughly exposing the Donation of Constantine, the Catholic Church **suppressed the information from the public** for centuries. One key often needed to prove guilt in a court of law is motive, and the **motive of Rome** has come loud and clear, straight from her own *"chair"* — all power, all authority, and all dominion on Earth, all in the name of God!

FLESHLY SCHEMES

Scripture admonishes true Believers not to resort to **fleshly schemes** for its increase, not to mention that the increase should be numbers of souls Saved from eternal Hell, not exponentially expanding dollars in the bank. Certainly, the early Church did not waste their energy seeking temporary gains, but as we will see, the Catholic Church has exhausted tremendous effort towards such.

In fact, the Bible says that, in this pursuit, many have erred from the faith; they left the pursuit of a heavenly Kingdom (the knowledge of Christ and the sharing of Christ) for the kingdoms of the world. *"Perverse disputings of men of corrupt minds, and destitute of the Truth,* **supposing that gain is Godliness***: from such withdraw thyself. But Godliness with contentment is great gain. For we brought nothing into this world, and it is certain we can carry nothing out. And having food and raiment let us be therewith content. But they that will be rich fall into temptation and a snare, and into many foolish and hurtful lusts, which drown men in destruction and perdition. For the* **love of money is the root of all evil***: which while some coveted after, they have* **erred from the Faith***, and pierced themselves through with many sorrows. But thou,* **O man of God, flee these things** *. . . Charge them who are rich in this world, that they be not highminded, nor trust in uncertain riches, but in the Living God, Who gives us richly all things to enjoy"* (I Tim. 6:5-11, 17).

Satan even tried to tempt Christ using the same appeal: *"Again, the Devil took Him up into an exceeding high mountain, and showed Him all the kingdoms of the world, and the glory of them; And said unto Him, All these things will I give You, if You will fall down and worship me"* (Mat. 4:8-9).

Notice **Satan's trade-off for the kingdoms of the world; you must worship him**, and if there is anything that constitutes a departure from the Faith, it is worshipping the Devil. Those who pursue the **dominion of earthly kingdoms** are literally selling their souls to Satan!

STEWARDSHIP

The Catholic "*church*" often uses the excuse that its amassment of wealth is done for the security of the sake of Christ. But, what does the spread of the Gospel of Jesus Christ have to do with the spread of business, territories, or social policy? **The spread of the Gospel is the spread of a Message!**

The truth is that the Roman Catholic Church is not interested in the spread of the Gospel. If they were, with the amount of money they have amassed, this whole world would have been saturated with the Good News by now. And since they claim all their money is for the cause of the Lord, at the very least they must be unbelievably bad stewards. "*And He said also unto His Disciples, There was a certain rich man, which had a steward; and the same was accused unto him that he had wasted his goods. And He called him, and said unto him, How is it that I hear this of You?* **give an account of your stewardship**; *for you may be no longer steward*" (Luke 16:1-2).

True stewardship always acts in favor of the Message because there is no hope and no help for humanity other than the Message of Jesus Christ and Him Crucified! The truth is, the Roman Catholic elite are liars, and they need to put their money where their mouth is!

Surely, this horrific waste of the money they claim is for God is enough evidence alone to prove that the fruit of Roman Catholicism is evil, not good. Poor stewardship is bad fruit. The Roman Catholic Church is a "*den of thieves!*" (Mat. 21:13). And the Book of Revelation clearly reveals what will happen to this modern Babylon who has committed fornication with the kings of the Earth for her own gain: "*And the kings of the earth, who have committed fornication and lived deliciously with her, shall bewail her, and lament for her, when they shall see the smoke of her burning, Standing afar off for the fear of her torment, saying, Alas, alas, that great city Babylon, that mighty city! for in one hour is thy judgment come*" (Rev. 18:9-10).

# CHAPTER FOURTEEN

THE EARLY CHURCH

The true Early Church fulfilled the teaching of Jesus Christ. As the saying goes, they practiced what they preached, their lifestyle clearly demonstrating the Faith they professed. Therefore, they strove to accumulate the riches and treasures of Heaven before the accumulation of those on Earth.

Following in the footsteps of the Apostles and in the true Spirit of the Lord, the Early Church had one goal — to hear and obey the Commandments of Christ. The price did not matter; they even abandoned their possessions when necessary. *"**And straightway they forsook their nets, and followed Him**"* Mk. 1:18). But this was not difficult because the Disciples truly believed that the riches of Heaven far outweighed the riches of Earth.

Still, having spiritual eyes, the Early Church could see that the beauty of God makes even the rarest and most precious diamond seem uninspiring. The beauty of Christ now living inside them was their living dream, and they knew that the richness of God was the treasure their heart had sought. Indeed, they could still see that the **riches of Heaven's Kingdom meant the inheritance of Christ — the Sonship of the Father**. In Christ, they had everything!

Members of the Early Church often sold or gave individual surplus for the benefit of the Body of Christ, so that even the poorest among them could be cared for through this **giving grace**. What a witness of the Lord's provision! The **Holy Spirit's reign** in their lives restrained personal attachment to riches so that wealth did not automatically bring selfishness. They functioned similar to a family; the blessing of one was a blessing to all, and in this way, the Church maintained the genuine apostolic tradition of putting

Heaven's Kingdom first, even until the Third Century when the Church's wealth had become substantial.

HUMAN GREED

However, it was not long until **human logic**, fueled by human greed, began to diffuse **childlike Faith** and love. The process of reasoning began, and the original teachings of the Disciples were eventually redefined. Having stifled and ignored significant passages of God's Word, **consensus established** that there was nothing wrong with clinging to earthly riches as long as they would be used for **religious purposes** (Manhattan, Avro. *The Vatican Billions*, p. 20).

Unfortunately, they failed to realize that the "*service of religion*" was not the same as serving Christ, and thus, a "*religion of Christ*" began to replace a true "*relationship with Christ.*" The church as a corporate body began to deliberately accumulate wealth, justifying its indulgence by the **good deeds** its money could provide. Believers also felt it was an honorable deed to leave money to the church since she had become the great commissioned hands, financially capable of **curing society's ills** and providing **aid to maintain the world**.

And meanwhile, this course of action made "*Christianity*" a respectable institution in the world system, a **savior for humanity's physical condition**. So, the church had traded the spiritual for the carnal, and accordingly, even the world began to love the "*good*" church.

Individual Christians also started to follow the example of their religious creation, no longer leaving their former lives to follow Christ. Instead, they began to **combine the two dichotomous kingdoms**, believing that the pursuit of worldly possessions was actually part of pursuing the Kingdom of God.

And although the Early Church shared their abundance with one another, no **religious hierarchy** was formed in order to administer it; the Spirit of the Lord kept every mouth fed (both physically and spiritually). The Roman Catholic Church, however, became the guardian of her followers' wealth, deciding when and how to distribute the privileges of her sons, each one upon his first baptism. **The *"Church"* had replaced the Holy Spirit.**

POLITICAL POWER

Not only did many in the world begin to look to the church to meet its physical needs, a few began to recognize its value for **political power** as well since the church had already won the **favor of the people**. Emperor Constantine chose to associate himself with the reputable Church, and thus, used this **positive social relationship** to further his popularity and cause.

Constantine officially recognizing the Christian Church in A.D. 313, and with the church on his side, he greatly furthered his governmental agenda. He effortlessly conquered the enemies of his dictatorial state. The church, in turn, enjoyed the protection of the state. What a deal! Who would not want such advanced security?

But sadly, dependence on the state only taught the church further **dependence on the ways of the world** rather than dependence on Christ. The Catholic Church, therefore, found it more and more necessary to **impress man**. It began to openly **display its status** with things such as **castle-like cathedrals** and **luxuriant wardrobes** for its clergy; clearly the church was no longer amassing money just to help the poor.

Their growing power and prestige also fostered another problem — **pride**. The Church Triumphant began to transform, ruin, or completely shut down pagan temples believing that **princes and princesses of the King deserved to rule**. They often turned such temples into so-called "*Christian*" shrines as they confiscated the property and wealth of the infidel, and non-Christian clergy began to find themselves without a job. Also, the Roman Catholic leaders enacted a swift policy to acquire real estate; high positions in government, commercial enterprises, etc., anything that would help them mingle with the world's elite (p. 21).

So, because the church allowed a preoccupation with money,

earthy pleasures, and the respect of the world to cloud their judgment, they ended up becoming a **key player on the world scene** rather than a light to it, and unfortunately, their social standing had become too high a price to pay to truly follow Jesus. Like the rich young ruler, they had too much to loose.

IDOLS

This phase of the church brought the great **tradition of pilgrimage**. Certain locations where the saints had lived, been martyred, or had been buried, were said to contain elements of spiritual cleansing and intensification. **Touring** these monasteries, nunneries, and churches of the saints and their miracle-working remains kept people coming from far and wide; everyone wanted the blessing of the supernatural. Not to mention, the **ancient mysteries imbedded within their halls** were irresistible to all **thrill seekers**.

This, of course, was really just another way for the Catholic Church to build its wealth and esteem since worshippers felt their **tangible experience** would be well worth any expense. In fact, the more spiritual benefit a particular shrine was said to provide, the more silver and gold coins regularly spilled from its altar (p. 23).

The truth is that while a life-changing experience may genuinely change your life, it does not automatically change your eternal life, and while you may reach the **mountain peaks** of this world, your soul may never emerge from the deepest **pit of Hell**. Your condition on Earth does not reflect your spiritual position.

Nevertheless, people still tend to trust what they can see, hear, and feel, making any **religiously-inclined activity** potentially dangerous. The pilgrimage to "*Peter's tomb*" easily became the chief expedition, since the Catholic Church blasphemously teaches that Peter (and his successor, the Pope) is essentially Christ on Earth, **Christ having turned over His keys to Peter**. Certainly, the burial site of the "*Blessed Peter*," the "*Turnkey of Heaven*" himself, would bring in the masses.

PETER?

Peter's tomb did bring thousands to the *"Eternal City of Rome"* and subsequently, millions into the treasury of Rome. In 1968, Pope Paul VI officially declared that *"a few fragments of human bones"* under the Basilica of St. Peter were the authentic remains of the Apostle Peter (*The Times*, London, June 26, 1968). One would have to wonder how Peter's bones had been distinguished on a site where hundreds of thousands of bodies had been buried for several centuries, but as to be expected, the Bishops of Rome did not feel the need to explain this. Rather, the **greedy leaders** chose to promote their lying legends that would bring in more wealth. It was easy; all they had to do was pretend to be commendable men of God holding fast to the so-called ***"truths"* intact within church history**, and at the same time, these scoundrels dismissed factual evidence disproving their **traditional myths**.

For example, there has never been any proof that Peter had ever been in Rome at all, much less crucified and buried there, but nevertheless, what appropriately became known as the ***"cult of Peter"*** demanded a **journey to Rome** where Peter supposedly lay. **Pilgrims** prayed over the Apostle's grave, believing in the immense righteousness they would receive for their efforts.

Pope Leo spoke of regulars like Emperor Valentinian III and his family who performed devotions there bringing with them costly gifts including gifts of land for the Church. Pope Gregory went a step further and offered Queen Brunhelda **remission of sin** as long as she gave him money, real estate, investitures, etc. He told her that *"The most blessed Peter, Prince of the Apostles . . . will cause thee to appear pure of all stain before the judge everlasting . . ."* (St. Gregory, *Letter 65*).

So, from the beginning, the **rich were given preferential treatment**, and this practice only got worse with time. Can you imagine Jesus giving the most blessings to those who could give Him the most in return? Can you see the Disciples showing favoritism to the highest tither? Of course not, because they knew it was God upon whom they were to rely for the necessary increase, not rich men.

GREED!

Pope Gregory's greed then began to take on a life of its own. He sent a nobleman, Dynamius, a cross containing something special — *"filings"* from Peter's chains! Gregory told Dynamius to wear the cross at his throat so that *"these chains, which have lain across and around the neck of the most blessed Apostle Peter, shall unloose thee for ever from thy sins"* (Willibald, *Vita Bonifacii*, 14).

How profane can one get, as if Peter's chains could loose anyone from sin. Rather, spiritually speaking, it was Christ's chains that loosened the chains of Peter as well as the chains of us all! I wonder if, in his wildest dreams, Pope Gregory ever thought he would be so controlled by money that he would make up something this pathetic. If the people had not been so spiritually blind as well, they would have seen what a fool his insatiable lust had made him. Gregory even began to send out *"the keys of St. Peter, wherein are found the precious filings and which by the same token also remit sins"* (St. Gregory, *Letters 12-17*).

Of course, Pope Gregory was not the only one who required payment for such items; none of the gifts from the demented line of Peter's successors were free. Something was always required in return. What a bad example of the Gospel of Jesus Christ! Everything we have from God is a gift!

Everything we have from God is free! **God freely gave** His Son, Jesus Christ, and Christ freely gave His Life for all the rest! Abraham told Isaac that the Lord would provide a Lamb, and He did! (Genesis 22:8) *"For God so loved the world, that He gave His only Begotten Son, that whosoever believes in Him should not perish, but have Everlasting life"* (Jn. 3:16). The Lord Jesus would later instruct His Church "... ***freely ye have received, freely give***" (Mat. 10:8).

THE OCCULT

Now, since St. Peter's successors (the popes) and St. Peter's relics both had the power to remit sins, the draw to Rome was even more difficult to resist. King Canute gave us a good example of the mindset a pilgrim to Rome might have had as he reflected on his own visit there, "... *I have done this because wise men have taught me that the Apostle Peter received of the Lord great power to bind and to loose, that he is the turnkey of the kingdom of Heaven ... That is why I thought it most useful to obtain the special patronage before God.*"

Thus, the pilgrimage was named the "*Pardon of St. Peter,*" and believers were even told they would be able to "*address the Blessed Peter in person.*" No wonder it was called the "*cult of Peter!*" Besides the Church having transferred Christ's authority to Peter, the people were taught they could actually commune with this dead saint!

The **contact of departed souls** is a marked characteristic of **occultist activity**, and clearly forbidden in Scripture! Any exchange made can only be demonic in nature as evil spirits pose as saints in order to further deceive the poor person.

In "*De Gloria Martyrum,*" St. Gregory of Tours gave a detailed description of the **ritual** one would perform in order to speak to the Prince of Apostles. The procedure asked the pilgrim to **kneel** upon Peter's tomb, insert his head through the trap door of the tomb, and, remaining in that same posture, reveal his requests to the corpse in a loud voice. Apparently, being dead, made St. Peter a little hard of hearing. How stupid! Can you imagine any sane individual thinking he could actually speak loud enough to **wake the dead**? The dutiful pilgrim would then be asked to toss some more money directly into the grave. This, too, should have been a pretty good clue that something was not quite right, but then again, if you're determine to **throw away money**, I guess a grave is as good a place as any. Finally, the pilgrim would have to **venerate another idol** — of course being none other than, the Pope as St. Peter's successor (p. 25).

See, the truth is that leaders of the Catholic Church hook their followers into a demonic stranglehold causing irrationality and an

inability to think for one's self, all in order for Rome to remain a prosperous world competitor. It is a fact that, for her own purposes, the Roman Church used the world and even her own people while telling both these victims that their activity was **scoring points with God. Are you serving God or your church**?

CHAPTER FIFTEEN

ST. PETER'S PATRIMONY?

Since the early church chose to trade a Heavenly Kingdom for an earthly kingdom, the resulting abundance of wealth soon required protection. The church, therefore, began to develop a **system of church order** (outside the Biblical model), which unfortunately, continues to be the foundation upon which Catholicism maintains her wealth today. Naive followers of the early church ended up contributing much time, effort, and money toward the fulfillment of **church objectives** which were never truly instigated by the Lord, all because they forgot to consult the Lord on their own. Constantine's decree proclaiming the right and responsibility of the church to **acquire foreign lands for Christ** was just one of many orders giving the people what they believed was sufficient justification for their absent-minded contribution. The church treasury became the perpetual inheritance of the succeeding Bishops of Rome as these leaders would make all the decisions regarding the use of *"God's property"* to further what was now seen as *"God's kingdom."* This **global estate** would come to be known as *"St. Peter's Patrimony."*

But to say that Christ is the Lord of one's life means that Jesus rules and Jesus reigns! It means **Jesus is King, not St. Peter and his successors**! It means that a person has surrendered to God by way of Christ's Cross, and God is now the decision-maker in his life, not the *"wise men"* of the church. **How can you call Christ your Lord, when you answer to men?** If the true Lordship of Christ operates within you, both man and religion are out of the picture! Christianity is an **individual walk of Faith** that trusts in the Lord's guidance, even when the group chooses to **ride another wave**.

ROADBLOCK TO THE CROSS

Corrupt leadership can easily take advantage of one's lack of personal relationship with Christ. For instance, during the earliest time of **transformation to church order**, even clergy of lesser rank began collecting money for the performance of sacraments (another unscriptural law helping to insure church wealth), and some even took the opportunity to make side money off of church goods during this time of weak individual faith.

You are responsible for your own salvation! The Bible says to, *"Trust in the LORD with all your heart; and lean not unto your own understanding. In all your ways acknowledge Him, and He shall direct your paths" (Prov. 3:5-6)*. Surely, when we acknowledge the Lord, by way of Christ's Cross, we can walk with Christ.

But, when a third party is allowed to dictate God's direction to us, **a walk of Faith transforms into a walk of Law**, and we are at the mercy of those positioned above us. This is exactly the scenario of the Catholic believer. **Church law becomes a roadblock to the Cross** and, therefore, **a roadblock to Christ's Lordship** as well. The individual cannot really live for God!

Pope Gregory was the first to officially investigate the total status of the Patrimony; this became the first complete census of the church's assets. He began to require every **Christian community** to make an **inventory** of all its sacred vessels, lands, and properties. Pope Gregory himself was shocked to see just exactly how rich *"St. Peter's Patrimony"* had become.

Only 300 years after Constantine, Roman Catholicism had already turned herself into the largest land owner in the West, taking in the combined revenue of over one million dollars a year. It owned twenty-three estates whose total area consisted of three-hundred and eighty square miles. It was clear that the church no longer kept just a modest sum to help the needy; she was now an economic success whose ever-increasing bank account had nearly made her invincible.

AN EARTHLY KINGDOM NEEDS AN EARTHLY ARMY

But, as with all material possessions, there are no guarantees. The Bible warns about **treasures thieves can steal**. *"Lay not up for yourselves treasures upon Earth, where moth and rust does corrupt, and where thieves break through and steal"* (Mat. 6:19). And indeed, the popes finally did encounter a serious scare.

During the Eighth Century, Arabs began to raid St. Peter's Patrimony. In the name of their God, Allah, they began to steal Papal possessions and demand that laymen and clergy alike convert to the Muslim faith. Through fear of death, many did change religions, and as a result, whole papal dominions were lost including Dalmatia, Istria, Spain, the South of France, and the whole of North Africa. Shortly after these invaders, the Lombards of North Italy set out to rob St. Peter as well.

It was at this point that the current pope realized he must do something drastic to save **St. Peter's kingdom**, so he decided to invoke the help of none other than the Blessed Peter himself. Pope Stephen decided that he must ask St. Peter to mobilize the most powerful potentate of the times, Pepin, the King of the Franks to defend the church and preserve her possessions. Now, apparently, the church needed a militia! **An earthly kingdom needed an earthly army**. Not surprisingly, Pope Stephen claimed that the Blessed Peter was in complete agreement with his **un-Christlike plan of war** and immediately **granted his wish**.

Is it any wonder he would rather invoke the help of a familiar spirit (disguised as St. Peter) than the Lord? False spirits tend to help us advance our own ideas and strategic plans while the Lord sovereignly gives us His Will and asks us to walk by Faith.

As the story goes, St. Peter wrote a letter for Pope Steven, direct from Heaven, to King Pepin! Naturally, the **letter from Heaven** would be delivered to Pope Stephen rather than Pepin, but the people would easily accept this absurdity since they had already been conditioned to expect their instruction from Heaven to come through popes, priests, or other *"holy"* fathers. They were already used to having a relationship with God through all kinds of **idolatrous intermediaries**.

And surely, St. Peter's letter was stunningly designed — written in **pure gold** on the finest vellum available. The people would certainly think anything so **angelically beautiful** had to be from God. The leaders also knew that if they gave the letter a **flashy presentation** and plenty of **hype** it would help the people believe despite the unbiblical and unrealistic nature of the **celestial message**. Obviously, there could not have been any physical evidence that St. Peter's letter had come from God, and if anything *"real"* had happened at all, it would have been obtained using witchcraft (summoning a spirit)!

This is much like the countless **apparitions of Mary** and her messages from Heaven that people follow all across the world today! What's next? — UFOs and messages from aliens? The Lord said, *"My sheep hear My voice, and I know them, and they follow Me"* (Jn. 10:27). Whose voice are you listening to? Only One should matter.

THE FALSE LETTER

The **false letter from the *"Prince of the Apostles"*** began as follows:

> *"Peter, elected Apostle by Jesus Christ, Son of the Living God. I, Peter, summoned to the apostolate by Christ, Son of the Living God, has received from the Divine Might the mission of enlightening the whole world... Wherefore, all those who, having heard my preaching, put it into practice, must believe absolutely that by God's order their sins are cleansed in this world and they shall enter stainless into everlasting life. Come ye to the aid of the Roman people, which has been entrusted to me by God. And I, on the day of Judgment, shall prepare for you a splendid dwelling place*

in the Kingdom of God.

Signed, Peter,
Prince of the Apostles"

Could this letter have implied that the Roman people and those who would align with her were somehow **chosen of God**? If so, this is a dangerous thought because during this Church Age, again, just like Salvation, the Lord deals with us on a personal basis. The Lord protects every child that is truly His no matter what nationality, race, age, or gender. As long as the person repents of sin and **believes in the New Covenant** (which is Faith in Jesus as the Messiah and His atoning Work on the Cross), God protects him in this life and in the next. But, if not, Hell awaits. All have sinned, and all will be judged if the Blood of the Lamb has not been applied to the doorpost of the heart! **We must not face death thinking our nationality has saved us!**

The Papal Envoy swore to the legitimacy of St. Peter's letter as he displayed the dazzling **extra-biblical epistle** before the whole court of King Pepin and described its incredible advent. He testified that the Blessed Peter appeared in person, having descended from Heaven, to deliver the letter to his trusted successor, the pope of Rome. He also vouched for the authenticity of Peter's signature, claiming that St. Peter had, in fact, written the whole letter by his very own hand! **King Pepin reverently knelt before the Roman officer** as he read these words from Peter, and just as hastily, Pepin bowed to all requests of the letter as well. St. Peter had supposedly addressed the message as follows:

"Peter, elected Apostle by Jesus Christ, to our favorite Son, the King Pepin, to his whole army, to all the bishops, abbots, monks, and to the whole people."

Did you notice the **flattering words of persuasion** towards King Pepin, calling him "*our favorite son*"? This should have been a total giveaway that the letter was a fraud. Jesus and His Disciples did not use any form of manipulation: "*For neither at any time used* *we flattering words...*" (I Thess. 2:5). Would Pepin earn more of the Lord's favor if he protected the Roman church? This was certainly what Pope Steven wanted him to believe, but unfortunately, for Pepin, the truth was probably the exact opposite. While he may earn the favor of the church, he would earn the curse of God since the Roman church was not operating in proper relationship with the Lord. In his *Historia Ecclesiastica*, the commended Fleury could not contain his indignation at the Blessed Peter's letter which he declared to be "*an unexampled artifice.*" However, the letter accomplished exactly what it was meant to.

In 754, Pepin defeated the Lombards, turning over all preserved and recovered lands to the church. He added the Duchy of Rome, the Exarchate, and Pentapolis. The total area of territories was quite considerable, including thousands of villages, forts, cities, farms, and estates which, from that day forward, would be owned by the representatives of St. Peter on Earth, the popes of Rome.

In 774, Pepin's immediate successor, Charlemagne, confirmed Pepin's Donation to Rome. By this point, the Papal States had, indeed, become a concrete and accepted reality. The popes continued to reign, each as **absolute ruler of church and state** for more than a thousand years, until 1870 when the Italians finally seized Rome and its adjacent papal territories, declaring Rome the capital of the United Kingdom of Italy.

FLEECING THE PEOPLE

Indeed, the vast power and prestige of the Roman Catholic Church was **built upon the forged documents and ungodly decretals of the papacy which were used to fleece the people!** Remember, the people lacked an intimate knowledge of the Lord, and so they were left to play "*follow-the-leader*" just like helpless little children. The Lord had forewarned His people about this very thing: "*My people are destroyed for lack of knowledge...*" (Hos. 4:6).

And another example of **liturgical false shepherding** came right after Pepin's death. This time the alleged *"communications between Pepin and the successor of the Turnkey of Heaven, the Blessed Peter"* were said to have been found. This would serve as a proof that Pepin had donated to the pope, not only Rome and the Papal States already mentioned, but also Istria, Venetia and indeed the whole of Italy (*Fables and Prophecies of the Middle Ages*, Dollinger). Even the Donation of Constantine, which was probably the forgery used by Pope Hadrian I to persuade Charlemagne to comply with the church, had been preceded by various forged documents of the papacy which were all said to have been the unmistakable directives of the Blessed Peter. You see, the newly born Papal States concluded they were too small to represent St. Peter; they decided their territories should be extended to match **Peter's spiritual supremacy**, and so the objective of the laymen should always be to obtain more power, territory, and wealth for Peter's line of successors.

In the mean time, the people had become so **proud of their religion**, they thoroughly enjoyed the fact that their popes lived like kings because, from their perspective, the **prosperity of the leaders justified the whole system**. They tragically believed that if the leaders were richly blessed, it was a sign that the faith they followed was approved by God.

THE POPE

The **Donation of Constantine** may be considered the most effective of the forgeries as it put popes above kings, emperors, and nations. In the first clause, the pope became the legal heir of Constantine, meaning the legal heir to the entirety of the Roman Empire. The second clause gave him **dominion over all Christendom**, meaning the East, West, and all churches of the world. With the third, he became the **one and only judge of Christian belief**, meaning that any person or any church who disagreed with his interpretation of Scripture, including what he believed regarding secular governance, was labeled and **punished as a heretic**!

The Donation of Constantine spoke clearly of the pope's supremacy, both the temporal and the spiritual, giving him sufficient authority to **restructure societies and political frameworks** during the Middle Ages. The Donation had first appeared in 754 at the Abby of St. Denis where Pope Stephen had spent the winter, providing some evidence that Stephen was personally involved in its fabrication, but it is also quite possible that the Donation may have been forged as early as 753 and simply brought by Stephen to the court of Pepin in 754 to help persuade him to give the popes their first territorial possessions.

Once the Papal States had officially come into being, the document was concealed until the opportune time to present to Pepin's son, Charlemagne *(Realencyclopadie*, G.H. Bohmer). Charlemagne also granted additional territories to the Papal States, and in the year 800, he was crowned by Pope Leo at St. Peter's in Rome, as the first Emperor of the Holy Roman Empire.

ABOVE THE LAW

And yet another set of forgeries, complementary to the Donation, appeared about a half century later. In 850, the "***Pseudo-Isidorean Decretals***", better known as the "***False Decretals***", made their first official manifestation. This heterogeneous collection of decrees from several earlier councils and popes appeared to provide some legal justification toward the complaints of some clergy members. The "*Decretals*" were supposed to have been official appeals to Rome regarding the misdeeds of civil authorities. Some of them may have been genuine, but the majority were fabricated in order to solidify the power of Roman Catholic Papacy by giving the abbots, bishops, and clergy in general, "*authority over civil jurisdiction in all provinces.*"

In other words, now the Papacy could operate **above the law**! Using the Decretals, the Roman Church was **dismissed from all local courts and all retribution by secular authority**! Thus, through a series of false documents, containing **false** "*words from God*," the popes not only gained control of the world financially, but governmentally as well. At every opportunity, they used their mounting omnipotence to weaken civil government throughout the nations, including even the power of kings and emperors! **The Papacy wholeheartedly believed that world dominion should belong to them as the *"vicars of Christ"* on earth!**

CHAPTER SIXTEEN

A DEPARTURE FROM THE WORD OF GOD

"The Priests did not ask, 'Where is the Lord?' Those who deal with the Law did not know Me; the leaders rebelled against Me. The Prophets prophesied by Baal, following worthless idols" (Jer. 2:8).

The face of evangelicalism has been changed by two major campaigns popularly known as the *"market driven church"* and the *"Purpose Driven Life"* (*PDL*), based on Rick Warren's #1 New York Times Bestseller. In future generations, these movements will come to be known for their unprecedented evasion of Scriptural authority! Why? Because we see that the recent shift in the evangelical church, which has been flourishing by these programs, has actually become a **revolutionary overthrow of true spiritual authority!** The authority for what the church has always believed — meaning *"the authority of the Bible"* — has changed! The basis for understanding the church's life and purpose has shifted from God's Word to psychological/sociological expertise, trends of pop-culture, business savvy, and an overlying philosophy of pragmatism (that truth is preeminently to be tested by practical results, that the *"end justifies the means"*).

MANIPULATION OF THE WORD

While these movements have never denied the Bible itself, they regularly deny it in much more subtle ways. They mistranslate it, misquote it, abuse its meaning, or attach sections of it to their own philosophies giving the appearance that Scripture backs their thinking. These manipulations erode the Power of God's Word and give the appearance that taking Scripture at face value isn't really that important. We are swiftly heading toward a Christianized community which has little use for the Bible rather than a community of true born-again Christians who live ". . . *by every word that proceeds out of the Mouth of God*" (Mat. 4:4).

Notice the widespread phenomena of people coming to church services without their Bibles; notice how sermons are being reduced to streamlined Power-Point presentations and presented with pre-made fill-in-the-blank note cards for the listeners. Thus, the Church has become a "*Christianity*" devoid of the Majesty of God and the Wonder of His Word!

THE THREE-LEGGED STOOL

We are now being told about five major problems facing the world, which are so huge that so far everyone has failed to solve them; even the United States and the United Nations. Nobody has brought down the **five global giants of** "*spiritual emptiness,*" "*egocentric or corrupt leadership,*" "*poverty,*" "*disease,*" **and** "*illiteracy.*" **Here is where Rick Warren presents the solution — "a *three-legged stool.*"**

Warren has said: "*For the stability of a nation, you must have strong healthy government, strong healthy businesses, and strong healthy churches. A three-legged stool will have stability. So I'm going from country to country teaching business its role, teaching church its role, and teaching government leaders their role — you've got to work together! We cannot solve the problem in your country or in the world if we won't work together*" (Philippine Daily Inquirer, July 30, 2006).

The three-legged stool is a concept developed and popularized by Peter Drucker, management guru and one of Rick Warren mentors. In fact, most all of the Purpose-Driven happenings can best be attributed back to Drucker's management philosophies — and not the Word of God. However, not surprisingly, these philosophies do fit quite nicely into the international plan for a new world order. "**Think global, Act local**" has been the mantra of the international globalist community ever since the early 1970's, and the role of the church in this system is:

1. To become a *"universal distribution"* system for health care, business development, teaching literacy, etc.;
2. To become the *"largest volunteer force"* in the world; and,
3. To seize upon its greatest asset, which Rick Warren claims is *"local credibility"* in every village.

PAGAN MYSTICISM!

In other words, the church **is to serve as the *"center"* or *"hub"* of the community, which networks and collaborates with government agencies and corporate entities in order to achieve a so-called *"healthy society."*** But what and who defines *"healthy"* as used in these management philosophies? All modern-day management theories are geared to create better *"workers"* for the global community and economy. These theories are derived from the social sciences, anthropology, psychology, sociology, and upon digging a little deeper, we find that many are actually **rooted in pagan mysticism**!

None of these concepts have anything to do with Scripture; they are all rather psycho-social in nature, and now they are being widely exported on a global scale. Sadly, thousands of pastors worldwide are being trained by Rick Warren in these humanistic models under the guise of *"Christianity."* The three-legged church is not about the Gospel of Jesus Christ!

As you can see, the **Church in this model becomes a social welfare agency**, an arm of both the corporate and state and a *"**global distribution network**."* Thus, the church has become a useful tool for those who have other purposes in mind, and we see that their plans are to **blend all religions into one acceptable religion worldwide! And what better way to do this than through mysticism since all religions, with the exception of true Christianity, have a mystic side to them. The Roman Catholic mystics and their mystical practices including contemplative prayer, breath prayer,** *lectio* *divina*, the stations of the cross, labyrinths, enneagrams, yoga, drumming, taize, etc., are already invading the true church!

RELIGIOUS MYSTICISM AND BIBLICAL SPIRITUALITY

It is obvious that a trend toward ecumenical unity and reconciliation is most fashionable within the modern church today, and mysticism is surely one of the most effective ways it is being accomplished. Mysticism deceptively focuses people upon a shared, personal **religious experience** with God, which appears to supercede doctrinal disputes. But keep in mind that bypassing doctrine means you must bypass the Word of God, and ignoring God's Word will only lead to a spirit world apart from God. *"It would seem that there are many professing evangelicals today who fail to understand the difference between religious mysticism and biblical spirituality"* (Morrison, Alan. *The Evangelical Attraction to Mysticism.*)

At one time, however, mysticism was openly and unsympathetically opposed by those wishing to save their brothers in Christ from mysticism's deadly deceptions. According to *The Zondervan Dictionary of Cults, Sects, Religions, and the Occult*, "*Mysticism has had outspoken opponents — mostly from Protestant circles, who maintain that it was a **derivative of ancient paganism and Gnosticism because it diverts attention away from the Gospel***" (Mather, G.A. & Nichols, Larry A. eds., 1993, p.201).

The infiltration of the Babylonian pagan religion into the church of Rome brought mystic practices right along with the rest of their pagan doctrines and idol-worship. We will later see how that the Roman Catholic monastic system provided a welcome home. But let's first look at what mysticism actually involves.

MYSTICISM IS AN ATTEMPT TO REACH GOD WITHOUT COMING TO THE CROSS OF CHRIST

It is somewhat difficult to concisely define mysticism. One scholar explains it as the search for ***unio mystica*, personal union**

with God (Moynahan, Brian. *The Faith*, 2002, p.269).

Another describes it this way: *"The mystic believes that there is an absolute and that he or she can enjoy **an unmediated link** to this absolute in a **superrational experience**"* (Corduan, Winfried. *Mysticism: an Evangelical Option*, 1991, p.32). There *". . . are at least three distinct categories of mysticism: panenthenic, in which, as* **Carl Jung** *thought, a segment of the **collective unconscious intrudes, on the conscious mind**; monistic such as found in Hinduism and Buddhism whereby the **individual is merged into the impersonal All**, whatever that is called: and theistic in which the absolute is God, although not necessarily the true God"* (p.45-46).

Professor Ferguson, the Dean of Open University and an advocate of mysticism, states that *"First, mystics believe that there is an Ultimate Being, a dimension of existence beyond that experienced through the senses . . . [which] is often, though not invariably, conceived in personal terms and called God . . . Second, mystics claim that the Ultimate can in some sense be known or apprehended . . . Third, the soul perceives the Ultimate through inward sense . . . Fourthly, it would be widely held by mystics that there is an element in the soul akin to the Ultimate, **a divine spark** . . . a holy spirit within. In this way, to find God is to find **one's true self** . . . Fifth, mysticism has as its zenith the experience of union with the Ultimate . . . The mystic seeks to pass out of all that is merely phenomenal, out of all lower forms of reality, to become Being itself"* (*An Illustrated Encyclopedia of Mysticism and Mystery Religions*, Thames & Hudson, 1976, p.127).

To sum it all up, one might say that **mysticism is an attempt to reach God without coming to the Cross of Christ!** Man is separated from God by sin, not a lack of spiritual knowledge, union, or consciousness! And it was only the Cross which once and for all bridged that great gulf between God and man called sin!

WHATEVER IS NOT OF FAITH IS SIN

There are three basic phases in the **journey of the mystic**:

purgation, illumination, and union. A basic understanding of the mystical journey will help us identify mysticism's ideology and practices, which have managed to creep into segments of the church from the earliest times. (The stages do not necessarily have to follow this exact order.) While the average practitioner may never fully experience all stages, the true mystic will strive to reach the maximum impact of the entire process.

Keep in mind, though, that the Bible teaches no process in which man plays any role except to have faith: "...*for whatsoever is not of faith is sin*" (Rom. 14:23). And, what is the faith? Trust in God's Grace for the accomplishment of one's entire existence in Him. This most certainly includes the process of sanctification, which we will see becomes very important in avoiding the trap of mystic ideology.

The first stage of mysticism, *Purgation*, involves the **works-oriented idea** that through some sort of physical suffering and/or **denial of fleshy pleasures** and material things one can attain holiness. Supposedly a **forced detachment from the world** will cleanse you and prepare you to experience more of God, even though this type of thinking is a direct denial of the Blood of Jesus. Often the stage of purgation begins with an intense self-examination in order to further rid "*self*" of its harmful hang-ups, which supposedly only keep the person attached to earthly concerns.

For instance, Sixteenth-Century monk, St. John of the Cross, is best known for his description of purgation which he calls the "*dark night of the soul*," and during this shadowy time of soul-searching, the person will usually experience a point of despair or abandonment by God. In modern psychiatry, this point may be called a "*catharsis.*"

DISCIPLES WITHOUT THE CROSS

The second stage, *Illumination*, begins to emerge from *purgation* in which the individual begins to see "*spiritually*," coming to know transcendent "*truths*," "*realities*," or "*God*" through non-rational means. In other words, mystics believe that the normal senses and reason cannot understand God (including the rational study of Scripture); you must be illuminated to see things in the spirit realm. The mystic often experiences **inner voices or visions** at this time, which they mistakenly consider to be insight from God. Mystics try to achieve illumination through fasting, ritualistic prayer, and other various **spiritual disciplines**. Some of the best of these disciplines were designed by the Catholic monk and founder of the Jesuits, Ignatius Loyola.

In fact, Richard Foster, who is widely respected among the evangelical community, despite his background as a Quaker/*"inner light"* mystic, patterns his book, *The Celebration of Disciple*, upon Loyola's *"Spiritual Exercises."* The *Celebration of Discipline* has been endorsed by many including Willow Creek, Dallas Willard, Youth Specialties, Focus on the Family, Abilene Christian University, and Regent University. Eugene Peterson, author of The Message Bible translation, had said that Richard Foster has *". . . found the spiritual disciplines [in the mystics] that the modern world stored away and forgot, and has excitedly called us to celebrate them"* (book review on *Celebration of Discipline*. Gary Gilley, p.206).

BE SOBER

We inevitably find, as well, that the majority of these spiritual practices attempt to put one in an altered state of consciousness attempting to uncover some buried knowledge trapped in our subconscious mind. This is a distinct trait of mysticism, that it always *". . . involves the utilization of certain practices in order to bring about **an altered state of consciousness** so that the person cannot only personally experience the Divine presence — however that may be perceived — but actually become unified with the Divine Essence, usually in a stupendous ecstatic experience"* (Morrison).

These mind-altering disciplines are largely entering the modern church today under the guise of *"contemplative prayer,"* *"spiritual formation,"* *"meditation,"* *"Christian counseling,"* and even *"extreme worship."* What's really scary about this is that the subconscious mind brings information that is not reality! Dreams are a result of an altered state of consciousness, but they are not real! Drugs alter your mind and senses as well, but drug-induced inspirations and/or hallucinations are not messages from God.

The Bible implores believers over and over again to "***Be Sober***". The Christian should be in his right mind at all times. *"Be sober, be vigilant; because your adversary the Devil, as a roaring lion, walks about, seeking whom he may devour"* (I Pet. 5:8). *"But let us, who are of the day, be sober, putting on the breastplate of Faith and Love; and for an helmet, the Hope of Salvation"* (I Thess. 5:8).

CHAPTER SEVENTEEN

The final stage of mysticism is called *Union.* A human soul is said to attain oneness with God due to having fully given himself over to the One (God) (Harkness, Georgia. Mysticism, 1973, p.32). It must be understood that this *"union"* or *"oneness"* with God occurs without a mediator. Considering that sinful man needs the Mediator, Christ Jesus, both now and forever, what could be more blasphemous? And furthermore, man can never attain the perfection necessary to be part of God's essence.

In his book, *The Inner Eye of Love: Mysticism and Religion,* the Roman Catholic monk, William Johnston says, *"It is a journey toward union because the* **consciousness gradually expands and integrates data from the so-called unconscious while the whole personality is absorbed into the great mystery of God***"* (p.127).

This thinking also leads to the idea that *"**all is one**"* because if everyone becomes one with God that also makes us one with one another. Ancient mystics often described this union with God in romantic, sensual terms. St. John of the Cross *"describes the union in terms of spiritual betrothal, where the soul, conceived of as feminine, is married to Christ as the bridegroom"* (Corduan, Winfried. p.35).

Even more disturbing, mystics teach that this point of *union* is actually where Christ is birthed in the soul. How much more can you pervert a truly *"holy"* relationship with God than to imply that a spiritually procreative experience with God creates his sons within us? Surely, the devil intends to construct no less than the vilest of blasphemies!

In one of his sermons, Johann Tauler, a Roman Catholic Dominican priest and teacher of mysticism, said that there were three ways

God was born in the Christmas season — the first birth is the Father begetting the Son, the second birth concerns maternal fruitfulness through virginal chastity and true purity, and the third birth happens when God is born within a just soul (Tauler, Johannes. *Sermons*. Paulist Press. 1985).

Where is any of this in the Bible? Nowhere. The Word of God no longer defines Christianity. **We have moved from allowing the Bible to define our spiritual experiences to allowing our experiences to define the Bible!**

MYSTICK ILLUMINATION

It is also very unfortunate that some of Tauler's experiences of mystic illumination were said to be the same experience of those in the Pentecostal movement — that of receiving the Baptism with the Holy Spirit. But, this is quite an outrageous claim considering the theology of the mystics was never Biblical and the Pentecostal experience, on the other hand, is clearly proclaimed in Scripture.

The Baptism with the Holy Spirit is Biblically Sound Doctrine! Praise God! This is one experience, like that of a sinner's glorious and miraculous Salvation in Christ Jesus, which is truly found in the Bible!

"And, being assembled together with them, Commanded them that they should not depart from Jerusalem, but wait for the Promise of the Father, which, said He, you have heard of Me. For John truly baptized with water; but you shall be baptized with the Holy Spirit not many days hence" (Acts 1:4-5).

"And suddenly there came a sound from Heaven as of a rushing mighty wind, and it filled all the house where they were sitting. And there appeared unto them cloven tongues like as of fire, and it sat upon each of them. And they were all filled with the Holy Spirit, and began to speak with other tongues, as the Spirit gave them utterance" (Acts 2:2-4).

CONTEMPLATIVE PRAYER

The rise of contemplative prayer in the church world today is astonishing! This type of prayer is the equivalent of Eastern meditative practices which teach one how to empty his mind and clear it of conscious thinking. This process usually begins with the use of a "***mantra***," a single word or syllable. The mantra is repeated or **chanted** over and over again until the person has found himself in certain stillness or quietness of mind, often called "***the silence***," but in reality, this is a relaxed trance-like state similar to hypnosis. Catholic mystics use **lecto divina** in which a particular verse of Scripture is focused upon and quoted repeatedly.

Contemplative prayer advocates say that this is the quieting of the mind needed in order to truly hear from God, but if this is so, I wonder why the Lord chose not to give us these instructions in Scripture, especially when the Disciples specifically asked Jesus to teach them "*how*" to pray! His lesson (the Lord's Prayer) does not even remotely resemble the contemplative prayer process. Instead, He gave them Faith-filled words of Truth with which to approach the Father and, interestingly, the Bible does specifically say "*But when you pray, use not vain repetitions . . .*" (Mat. 6:7).

One major promotion of this mystical meditation disguised as contemplative prayer, which has recently reached "*Christian*" bookshelves and, unfortunately, has even been endorsed by well-respected Christian authors such as Max Lucado and Beth Moore, is a new DVD called "*Be Still*", by Fox Home Entertainment. The title itself is the contemplatives' main attempt to use Scripture to justify their practice, but it is really a complete misinterpretation of Psalms 46:10. "*Be still*" means to rest — to trust — in the Lord whether one is being physically silent or not. And, there is certainly no indication of repetition of words. Once again, apostasy has come to the church through Catholicism.

Author Ray Yungen, who has studied religious movements specializing in New Ageism and Eastern religions for over 20 years, credits Thomas Merton, a Roman Catholic Trappist Monk, with being the first to make contemplative prayer available to the masses, taking it out of its original monastic setting (*A Time of Departing*, p.60). Thomas Merton has also been the mentor of several outspoken leaders in the modern church, including Emergent church leaders Richard Foster and Brian McLaren.

CATHOLIC MYSTICISM

As we mentioned earlier, much of mysticism's infiltration into the Catholic Church came through Catholic monks and nuns because they were attempting the exact same thing as the mystics — trying to attain a greater knowledge of God through a disconnect from the world even though this is works-righteousness and directly opposes the directives Christ gave His Disciples, which were to go and preach the Gospel unto the whole Earth! "*. . . You shall be witnesses unto Me both in Jerusalem, and in all Judaea, and in Samaria, and unto the uttermost part of the Earth*" (Acts 1:8).

While Christ wants Believers to separate from worldliness and sin, He never told Believers to isolate themselves from loved ones and society (which is actually a distinct characteristic of a cult). They weren't supposed to become useless gurus sitting on a mountain top!

The main origin of Catholic mysticism came when a Syrian monk wrote a number of theological treatises, which he said were actually written by "*Dionysius the Areopagite,*" who is briefly mentioned in the Book of Acts as a convert of the Apostle Paul (Acts 17:34). The Syrian monk was an advocate of "***via negativa,***" **the negative way**, whereby through **asceticism** and certain meditation practices one gradually eliminates all elements that are not divine.

This precisely follows the purgation stage of mysticism we discussed earlier. In fact, the two main themes of the pseudo-Dionysius are "*the exaltation of the 'via negative' above revealed theology*" and "*the doctrine of perfection by ecstasy*" (*Chamber's Encyclopedia* Vol. IV p.534). The pseudo-Dionysius also attempted to reconcile

Christianity with Neoplatonism which had pervaded the Greco-Roman culture of the time. This was a metaphysical system whose founder, Plotinus, also *"advocated asceticism and the contemplative life"* (Magnusson, Magnus ed., Chambers Biographical Dictionary, 1990, p.1172). Plotinus' well-known analogy describes a sculptor cutting away all that does not enhance the *"divine image."* It has been said that Neoplatonism *"provided the philosophical basis for the pagan opposition to Christianity in the Fourth and Fifth Centuries"* (Elwell, Walter J. *Evangelical Dictionary of Theology.* 1984, p.257).

Ungodly philosophies such as this, largely entered the church by way of **allegorical interpretations** of Scripture, providing heresy easy access to corrupt the Word. Actually, allegorical interpretation of sacred texts is another common element found among mystic religions; for instance, while the Sufis (Islamic mystics) would not deny the literal interpretation of the Koran, their emphasis was on a second symbolic meaning, and usually the help of a spiritual mentor is necessary to explain the deeper esoteric interpretation.

THE DESERT HERMIT

At one time, Christians found it necessary to hide from society. These were Christian **hermits** who lived in the Sahara desert of Egypt beginning in the Third Century. They were known as the **Desert Fathers**, and they were originally fleeing the persecution of Rome.

However, even after Christianity was made legal by Constantine in 313, some individuals chose to remain in this life of solitude, which they believed helped them develop stoic self-discipline, a character trait highly prized in Greco-Roman culture. They felt that John the Baptist was a model for their belief system as John, in their minds, was a desert hermit himself. They believed that the desert life would teach them to abstain from the things of the world so they could focus all their attention on seeking God. As a result, the deserts surrounding Egypt attracted many who wished to further develop their holiness and wisdom.

Over time, the hermits began to learn from one another until the generalized system began to develop which we know today as mysticism. One very notable Desert Father was John Cassian who eventually earned the title, *"bridge between the East and West"* (Stewart, Columba. *Cassian the Monk.* 1998). Having just left his time in the deserts of Egypt, he set up two new monasteries in southern Gaul in the early Fifth Century. Although these were not the only monasteries in Gaul, they were distinct in that they were based on the monastic system Cassian had grown to believe was a better representation of what true monastic life should be. He believed that the practical, ascetical, and mystical spirituality which had developed in Egypt provided the spiritual change (involving the gradual, forceful correction of faults and progression toward Christian perfection, *"vita perfecta"*) most closely reaching that the early Apostles experienced. Therefore, for Cassian, *"the life of the monk was the Apostolic life"* (Chadwick, Owen. *John Cassian.* 2nd ed. 1968). In essence, Cassian believed that the Egyptian monastic system was a representation of the Apostolic tradition itself, and he wished to establish that same system in the West. This fits into the Catholic system as well, since the lay people don't really try to know God on their own as much as they listen to their *"experts"* — their *"holy"* men and women who have supposedly gotten close to God in their mystic monasteries.

Modern emergent church leader Brian McLaren has stated that *". . . the emerging church must be 'monastic' — centered on training disciples who practice, rather than just believe, the faith . . ."* (*Christianity Today. The Emergent Mystique.* Nov. 2004.). This is quite an alarming statement because, as we have seen, **monastic discipleship is not Christian discipleship**.

Along with monastic discipleship, the call to celibacy in Catholic clerical tradition also fits into mysticism's teaching because one must first attain purity in order to unite with the divine. Since this law, however, is nowhere to be found in Scripture, it has only done the exact opposite of what it was meant to do throughout all pagan religions where the Babylonian-style order to priestly celibacy has been enacted including Tibet, China, Japan, and Pagan Rome. The evidence of its true effect on morality has been made more than obvious *(Hamel, Travels in Corea, Pinkerton Collection. Vol. vii).*

HISTORY

Throughout history, there have been revivals of mysticism in Catholicism. In the Twelfth and Thirteenth Centuries, many new orders of monks and nuns developed, influenced by the pseudo-Dionysius.

Then in the Sixteenth Century, we find mystics such as Ignatius Loyola, Teresa of Avila, and John of the Cross developing a more systematized process of mysticism. Their writings laid out more specific steps towards reaching unification with the divine, often describing the journey as an "*. . . ascent up a ladder or mountain, or down into the labyrinthine depths of the soul*" (Morrison).

Tragically, today's revival of mysticism has expanded beyond Catholicism into the Christian Church world, and we will be exposing more of this false spirituality and how it has infiltrated modern evangelical circles as we continue this study.

CHAPTER EIGHTEEN

While mystic practices are found among many different faiths, in a sense, mysticism constitutes a religion all in itself. It is **a religion based on *"experiences"* rather than beliefs.** It is wholly dependent on experience because experience is the very thing that is said to bring one into a greater knowledge of and communion with God. But do spiritual experiences automatically bring one closer to God? Are they automatically aligned with the God's Truth? Most assuredly, the answer is *"No."*

God gave us His Word with which to know His Truth, to experience true relationship with Him, and to judge all other things. **His Word is Truth!** Therefore, if any particular phenomenon is not found in the Bible, it did not come from the True God! One of the greatest errors proudly parroted in the modern church is *"all truth is God's truth,"* but this clever trick of Satan fails to explain that factual information is not the same as Biblical Truth. While it may be a fact that you had a mystical experience, it does not mean that you experienced Truth!

SPIRITUAL EXPERIENCES?

Now let's look a little closer at these spiritual *"experiences"* since many *"pastors"* in today's church have no problem promoting the mystic Catholic *"fathers"* who have mastered the practice. In fact, many undiscerning church leaders believe that some of the most adept *"experiencers"* are somehow **spiritual experts**, worthy to be granted positions of **authority**.

As we continue, you will soon see that the danger of such is beyond belief! It does no less than allow **psychic mediums** to become chief **spiritual advisors** to the church! The people, including the *"experiencers"* themselves, become deceived thinking their spiritual insights are from God when they are really a result of **divination**. *"There shall not be found among you any one who makes his son or his daughter to pass through the fire, or who uses divination, or an observer of times, or an enchanter, or a witch, or a charmer, or a consulter with familiar spirits, or a wizard, or a necromancer. For all who do these things are an abomination unto the LORD . . ."* (Deut. 18:10-12).

AN EMPTY MIND!

As we have discussed, a mystical experience comes as a result of an emptied mind that, in reality, puts the mind into an altered state of consciousness similar to hypnosis. The mystic uses methods such as contemplative prayer, meditation, yoga, **martial arts**, beating drums, focusing on a single object, mantra, etc. to **clear the mind**. The idea is that an empty mind has space to be filled, whereas a cluttered mind, full of **negative thinking** and the cares of the world, does not have the capacity to receive divine truths. **Apparently, the mystics believe that the Light of the Gospel cannot penetrate the darkness of the human soul; man must somehow clear the way first.** So-called *"Christian"* psychology often does exactly the same thing, thinking that by helping a person clean up his own life or overcome his own worries, he will be free to receive help from the Lord.

Secondly, the mystical experience is about power! As philosopher Sir Frances Bacon has well-stated, *"knowledge is power."* The mystic knows that enlightenment (or *"higher"* knowledge) will bring **empowerment**. Most important to the mystic is spiritual power, but the power can certainly include both the mental and physical as well. The natural man has very limited power, so if he wants more, he must get help from the spiritual realm. And indeed, the mystic fathers have had experiences that have actually empowered them, but the empowerment could not have come from the Holy Spirit because the Work of the Holy Spirit only comes through Faith in Christ's Cross. So, there is only one option left — these men have actually been endued with extra-special knowledge and ability by demonic spirits. **Mystical empowerment is Satanic empowerment!** You can even see this materialize in secular society as some of the most accomplished, motivated, talented, and innovative people in the world have been given just such empowerment.

EMPOWERMENT?

Some have not only received empowerment from other spirits but have actually met a few of these spirits as well. On occasion, a spirit appears as a peaceable **guide or teacher**, certainly nothing that would indicate its true nature. For instance, many have believed their spirit guide to be Jesus Himself. The Bible says the devil comes as *"an angel of light"* or a *"wolf in sheep's clothing."* In other words, he will appear to be good.

Helen Schucman, a Jewish atheistic psychologist from Columbia University, began in 1965 to channel messages from a spirit *"voice"* that she claimed identified itself as Jesus Christ. She produced a major work with his help over the course of seven years, which is now known as *A Course In Miracles*.

Believers such as Marianne Williamson, Dr. Gerald Jampolsky, and Robert Schuller have done their best to expose the church to this course, which supposedly brings a person into a realm of **miraculous experiences**. Unfortunately, its New Age terminology can sound somewhat like Christian terminology to the untrained ear (*The Holy Encounter*, Sept. 1989; taken from Contender Ministries on-line, "*A Course In Miracles*"). Believer, Marianne Williamson has been featured on the Oprah Winfrey Show and with Barbara Walters on the ABC television News Show 20/20 (*The Holy Encounter*, July/Aug. 1992, p. 2; July/Aug. 1993, p. 9).

Even the psychologist Carl Jung had a spirit guide named Philemon who gave Jung his renowned ideas regarding personality type upon which the Myers-Briggs Type Indicator is based!

Yes, many modern *"prophets"* are saying that the church is headed for a major *"paradigm shift,"* but they may not realize that this shift is a **shift to another spirituality** — one which will prepare the way for the coming antichrist. *"And deceives them who dwell on the Earth by the means of those miracles which he had power to do . . ."* (Rev. 13:14).

EXCHANGING BIBLICAL TRUTHS FOR MYSTICAL PRACTICES

David Jeremiah who currently pastors Shadow Mountain Community Church has recently endorsed a book called *The Barbarian Way* by Erwin McManus to help bring a *"major paradigm shift"* to his church (Shadow Mountain Community Church. *"Pastor's weekly message"* e-newsletter. 2005). Jeremiah is also the founder of Turning Point Radio and Television Ministries heard on over 1800 stations nationally and internationally.

In *The Barbarian Way*, McManus explains that the church needs to exchange reason (doctrine) for mysticism and become "***Mystic Warriors***." This is precisely what we have been talking about — exchanging Biblical Truths for mystic practices. McManus further explains that true followers of Christ need to become **warlike and passionate barbarians** in order to usher in the revival needed in today's church. His aggressive ideas become even scarier when he goes on to explain that the greatest enemy to his "***Jesus revolution***" is traditional Christianity, which he believes has become totally corrupt. In *The Barbarian Way*, McManus says, *"Two thousand years ago, God started to revolt against the religion He started. So don't ever put it past God to cause a groundswell movement against churches and Christian institutions that bear His name."* Essentially, McManus has declared **war on Christianity in the name of Jesus**!

A MYSTICAL VIEW OF CHRISTIANITY

David Jeremiah has also endorsed mystic practices in his 2003 book, *Life Wide Open: Unleashing the Power of a Passionate Life*, which tells readers how to *"bring real, living excitement into this life."* Here again, we see the all-important theme of *"experiencing"* something — more specifically, experiencing power to live a sensational life. He gives a list of those few he believes has discovered this secret which includes Erwin McManus, Rick Warren, Buddhist sympathizer Peter Senge (*The Fifth Discipline*), contemplative Sue Monk Kidd, contemplative Calvin Miller (*Into the Depths of God*), contemplative Michael Card, and Brother Lawrence (*Practicing the Presence of God*).

If Jeremiah believes that these contemplatives, several of whom do not even claim to be Christians, have realized the same passionate Christianity that he has written about in his book, his version of Christianity is mystical, not Biblical. Not to mention, we have already discussed what kind of spiritual empowerment contemplative mystics have attained!

Also, not surprisingly, this same idea of *"unleashing power"* is found in McManus', *The Barbarian Way*. McManus tells how a story of the **Crusades** *"awakens within me a primal longing that I am convinced waits to be unleashed within everyone who is a follower of Jesus Christ."*

Apparently, McManus has forgotten that the Crusades were never a result of truly following Jesus in the first place; the Crusades were a product of apostate Christianity, namely Catholicism.

NEW AGE THEOLOGY

Also, the very idea of *"**unleashing**"* or *"**awakening**"* one's *"**potential power**"* (whether to become a fierce warrior or simply to better one's life) has very definite connections to New Age theology (Lighthouse Trails Research Project e-newsletter. "*David Jeremiah Proposes 'Major Paradigm Shift' for His Church.*" September 2006). The New Age teaches that humans have a *"**divine spark**"* within them (which is God) that is just waiting to be released. Humans should realize their *"unlimited potential"* which is this *"god within"* and recognize that their goal in life is to *"awaken to the god who sleeps at the root of the human being"* (Maurice Smith. "*New Age Movement.*" *Interfaith Witness Belief Bulletin, May* 1988. p.2). Through teachers like Marianne Williamson, this New Age theology of *"**unlimited human** *potential*" has made its way through most all aspects of society as unsuspecting people are taught that "*you can do anything you put your mind to*" and "*never limit the power of your mind.*"

The Bible teaches the exact opposite — that the true "*self*" has no such power! The true Christian does not learn how to unleash **latent powers** of God; He learns to yield to the Holy Spirit through Faith in Christ's Finished Work on the Cross. Christians often confuse the New Age concept of a "*divine spark*" with the Biblical teaching that the Holy Spirit comes to dwell inside true Believers. The New Age "*god in you*" exists whether you know Christ as Savior or not. And while the Bible teaches that a Christian becomes like a tabernacle for Christ, the New Age teaches that the "*god within*" is actually "*a part*" of the "*self.*"

The Bible makes this distinction clear: "**For we preach not ourselves, but Christ Jesus the Lord**; *and ourselves your servants for Jesus' sake. For God, Who Commanded the light to shine out of darkness, has shined in our hearts, to give the Light of the Knowledge of the Glory of God in the Face of Jesus Christ.* **But we have this treasure in earthen vessels, that the excellency of the Power may be of God, and not of us**" (II Cor. 4:5-7).

OTHER MEDIUMS

Mystic teachings are influencing the modern church through **other mediums** as well. Take, for instance, Mel Gibson's **The Passion Of The Christ**. This movie's storyline was heavily influenced by the teachings of Saint Anne Catherine Emmerich, an Augustinian nun, stigmatic, and ecstatic, born September 8, 1774. In other words, St. Anne was a mystic and a very proficient one at that!

Her claims of her ability to communicate "*in the spirit*" with those who lived even centuries before her make the best of today's psychic readers look like amateurs. She says she has advised St. Peter's successor and even spoke to Jesus while he was a boy on Earth. "*Even in her childhood the supernatural was so ordinary to her that in her innocent ignorance she thought all other children enjoyed the same favors that she did, i.e. to converse familiarly with the Child Jesus."*

Saint Anne Catherine Emmerich wrote *The Dolorous Passion Of Our Lord Jesus Christ According To The Meditations Of Anne Catherine Emmerich*. Through these *"meditations,"* Emmerich presented to the world her version of what happened in the final days of the life of Jesus Christ. When Gibson uses **"*artistic license*"** for his description of the Passion, the **mystic additions** he inserts are largely taken from her writings. *"Her visions go into details, often slight, which give them a vividness that strongly holds the reader's interest **as one graphic scene follows another in rapid succession** as if visible to the physical eye. Other mystics are more concerned with ideas, she with events; others stop to mediate aloud and to guide the reader's thoughts, she lets the facts speak for themselves with the simplicity, brevity, and security of a Gospel narrative"* (Veneration of Anne Catherine Emmerich, New Advent Catholic Encyclopedia, on-line Ed.).

Doesn't it seem as if St. Anne's inspirational visions were always meant for cinema? Apparently, Mel Gibson thought so.

Emmerich's mystical experiences of **stigmata** are also completely demonic! *"Stigmata"* is when a human being takes on the physical, literal marks of the Passion of Christ. They may include nail prints, open scourging wounds in the hands, feet, and side, or wounds produced by the crown of thorns. Nowhere does the Bible mention any Christian having such horrific experiences that are often accompanied by visions, voices, and insights from the spirit world. You cannot obtain wisdom from God through physical suffering!